UNMANNED AERIAL SYSTEM THREATS: EXPLORING SECURITY IMPLICATIONS AND MITIGATION TECHNOLOGIES

HEARING

BEFORE THE

SUBCOMMITTEE ON OVERSIGHT AND MANAGEMENT EFFICIENCY

OF THE

COMMITTEE ON HOMELAND SECURITY HOUSE OF REPRESENTATIVES

ONE HUNDRED FOURTEENTH CONGRESS

FIRST SESSION

MARCH 18, 2015

Serial No. 114–9

Printed for the use of the Committee on Homeland Security

Available via the World Wide Web: http://www.gpo.gov/fdsys/

U.S. GOVERNMENT PUBLISHING OFFICE
WASHINGTON : 2015

94–580 PDF

COMMITTEE ON HOMELAND SECURITY

MICHAEL T. McCAUL, Texas, *Chairman*

LAMAR SMITH, Texas
PETER T. KING, New York
MIKE ROGERS, Alabama
CANDICE S. MILLER, Michigan, *Vice Chair*
JEFF DUNCAN, South Carolina
TOM MARINO, Pennsylvania
STEVEN M. PALAZZO, Mississippi
LOU BARLETTA, Pennsylvania
SCOTT PERRY, Pennsylvania
CURT CLAWSON, Florida
JOHN KATKO, New York
WILL HURD, Texas
EARL L. "BUDDY" CARTER, Georgia
MARK WALKER, North Carolina
BARRY LOUDERMILK, Georgia
MARTHA McSALLY, Arizona
JOHN RATCLIFFE, Texas

BENNIE G. THOMPSON, Mississippi
LORETTA SANCHEZ, California
SHEILA JACKSON LEE, Texas
JAMES R. LANGEVIN, Rhode Island
BRIAN HIGGINS, New York
CEDRIC L. RICHMOND, Louisiana
WILLIAM R. KEATING, Massachusetts
DONALD M. PAYNE, JR., New Jersey
FILEMON VELA, Texas
BONNIE WATSON COLEMAN, New Jersey
KATHLEEN M. RICE, New York
NORMA J. TORRES, California

BRENDAN P. SHIELDS, *Staff Director*
JOAN V. O'HARA, *General Counsel*
MICHAEL S. TWINCHEK, *Chief Clerk*
I. LANIER AVANT, *Minority Staff Director*

———————

SUBCOMMITTEE ON OVERSIGHT AND MANAGEMENT EFFICIENCY

SCOTT PERRY, Pennsylvania, *Chairman*

JEFF DUNCAN, South Carolina
CURT CLAWSON, Florida
EARL L. "BUDDY" CARTER, Georgia
BARRY LOUDERMILK, Georgia
MICHAEL T. McCAUL, Texas *(ex officio)*

BONNIE WATSON COLEMAN, New Jersey
CEDRIC L. RICHMOND, Louisiana
NORMA J. TORRES, California
BENNIE G. THOMPSON, Mississippi *(ex officio)*

RYAN CONSAUL, *Subcommittee Staff Director*
DENNIS TERRY, *Subcommittee Clerk*
BRIAN B. TURBYFILL, *Minority Subcommittee Staff Director*

CONTENTS

UNMANNED AERIAL SYSTEM THREATS: EXPLORING SECURITY IMPLICATIONS AND MITIGATION TECHNOLOGIES

Wednesday, March 18, 2015

U.S. House of Representatives,
Subcommittee on Oversight
and Management Efficiency,
Committee on Homeland Security,
Washington, DC.

The subcommittee met, pursuant to call, at 10:02 a.m., in Room 311, Cannon House Office Building, Hon. Scott Perry [Chairman of the subcommittee] presiding.

Present: Representatives Perry, Carter, Loudermilk, Watson Coleman, Thompson, Richmond, and Torres.

Mr. PERRY. Committee on Homeland Security Subcommittee on Oversight and Management Efficiency will come to order. The purpose of this hearing is to receive testimony regarding security implications of small, unmanned aerial systems in the domestic airspace and technologies to mitigate associated threats.

Chairman now recognizes itself for an opening statement.

When most people think of unmanned aerial systems, or UAS, commonly known as drones, they may think of large aircraft used in overseas combat operations. However, in the coming years, the majority of UAS will be small—55 pounds or less—many of which fly less than 400 feet above the ground. Small UAS have a variety of potential uses such as pipeline, utility, and farm inspections, aerial photography, and crop-dusting, among other uses.

Last month the Federal Aviation Administration, the FAA, released proposed rules to allow for the operation of small UAS for non-recreational purposes into domestic airspace. The proposed rules would place numerous limitations on flying small UAS: Flights could take place only in daylight, the area of operations would be limited, and only visual-line-of-sight operations would be permitted. These proposed rules are now open for public comment.

Our hearing today will focus on the security implications of opening our skies to small UAS and how agencies such as the Department of Homeland Security, Federal, State, and local law enforcement agencies should prepare.

Several recent security incidents are concerning. In January, a small quadcopter crashed on the White House lawn. Although the incident seemingly was accidental, it exposed the larger issue of how law enforcement should respond to UAS threats and, subsequently, the Secret Service quickly scheduled exercises in the D.C. area in response.

Also, a September 2013 incident where a small UAS landed only inches away from German Chancellor Angela Merkel also exposed serious concerns and the challenge that protective services around the world now face.

Last but not least, French police recently were confounded when several unidentified small UAS flew over key Paris landmarks, including the Eiffel Tower, as well as nuclear power plants. French authorities are investigating, but again, this incident showcases the challenges to law enforcement to respond swiftly to this new technology.

Threats posed by the small UAS are nothing new. For example, an individual was arrested in September 2011 after a failed plot to attack the U.S. Capitol and Pentagon using multiple remote-controlled aircraft laden with explosives.

But nightmare scenarios by terrorists aren't the only concern. Drug smugglers could use this technology as a cheap way to smuggle illegal drugs into the United States, and spies may also use small drones to get into areas we would prefer hidden.

So the question remains: How can homeland security and law enforcement prepare for these potential threats?

In July 2012, this committee held a hearing highlighting the need to address the security risks associated with UAS. In the past 3 years, the Department of Homeland Security has taken some steps to educate law enforcement and the public on small UAS.

The National Protection and Programs Directorate, the NPPD, released a model aircraft reference aid to inform the public about potential illicit uses, impacts, and indicators of malicious activity. The Science and Technology Director has been assessing the capabilities of small UAS for State and local law enforcement and first responders.

However, much more needs to be done to safeguard against malicious actors successfully using this technology for illegal means. The Department of Homeland Security needs a cohesive strategy to address these issues.

Lone-wolf terrorists, drug smugglers, and foreign spies don't care about FAA rules. The DHS must help protect against these bad actors perverting this technology for their objectives.

Testimony from our witnesses today will help provide a roadmap for what homeland security and law enforcement can do to mitigate this risk. Specifically, we need a better understanding of the technological solutions that exist to deal with these threats and what law enforcement needs to better respond when a small UAS is used for illegal activity.

I look forward to hearing from today's witnesses on their assessment of the threats and potential solutions.

[The statement of Chairman Perry follows:]

STATEMENT OF CHAIRMAN SCOTT PERRY

MARCH 18, 2015

When most people think of unmanned aerial systems (UAS), commonly known as "drones", they think of large aircraft used in overseas combat operations; however, in the coming years, the majority of UAS will be small—55 pounds or less—some of which fly less than 400 feet above the ground. Small UAS have a variety of potential uses, such as pipeline, utility, and farm inspections, aerial photography, and crop dusting, among others. Last month, the Federal Aviation Administration (FAA) released proposed rules to allow for operation of small UAS for non-recreational purposes into domestic airspace. The proposed rules would place numerous limitations on flying small UAS: Flights could take place only in daylight, the area of operations would be limited, and only visual-line-of-sight operations would be permitted. These proposed rules now are open for public comment. Our hearing today will focus on the security implications of opening our skies to small UAS and how agencies such as the Department of Homeland Security (DHS), Federal, State, and local law enforcement should prepare.

Several recent security incidents are concerning. In January, a small quadcopter crashed on the White House lawn. Although the incident seemingly was accidental, it exposed the larger issue of how law enforcement should respond to UAS threats and, subsequently, the Secret Service quickly scheduled exercises in the D.C. area in response. Next, a September 2013 incident where a small UAS landed only inches away from German Chancellor Angela Merkel also exposed serious concerns and the challenge that protective services around the world now face. Last but not least, French police recently were confounded when several unidentified small UAS flew over key Paris landmarks, including the Eiffel Tower as well as nuclear power plants. French authorities are investigating, but again, this incident showcases the challenges for law enforcement to respond swiftly to this new technology.

Threats posed by small UAS are nothing new. For example, an individual was arrested in September 2011 after a failed plot to attack the U.S. Capitol and Pentagon using multiple remote controlled aircraft laden with explosives. But nightmare scenarios by terrorists aren't the only concern. Drug smugglers could use this technology as a cheap way to smuggle illegal drugs into the United States, and spies may also use small drones to get into areas we would prefer hidden.

So the question is: How can homeland security and law enforcement prepare for these potential threats? In July 2012, this committee held a hearing highlighting the need to address the security risks associated with UAS. In the past 3 years, the Department of Homeland Security has taken some steps to educate law enforcement and the public on small UAS. The National Protection and Programs Directorate (NPPD) released a model aircraft reference aid to inform the public about potential illicit uses, impacts, and indicators of malicious activity. The Science and Technology Directorate has been assessing the capabilities of small UAS for State and local law enforcement and first responders. However, much more needs to be done to safeguard against malicious actors successfully using this technology for illegal means. The Department of Homeland Security needs a cohesive strategy to address these issues.

Lone-wolf terrorists, drug smugglers, and foreign spies don't care about FAA rules. DHS must help protect against these bad actors perverting this technology for their objectives. Testimony from our witnesses today will help provide a roadmap for what homeland security and law enforcement can do to mitigate this risk. Specifically, we need a better understanding of the technological solutions that exist to deal with these threats and what law enforcement needs to better respond when a small UAS is used for illegal activity. I look forward to hearing from today's witnesses on their assessment of the threats and potential solutions.

Mr. PERRY. The Chairman now recognizes the Ranking Minority Member of the subcommittee, the gentlelady from New Jersey, Mrs. Watson Coleman, for her statement.

Mrs. WATSON COLEMAN. Thank you very much, Mr. Chairman. Again, thank you for holding this hearing.

I would also like to thank the panel of witnesses for appearing before the subcommittee today.

I am very interested in hearing from Professor McNeal, an expert on the issue of drones, about the potential policy options available to mitigate and respond to the threats posed by the commercial availability of unmanned aerial systems. Additionally, I am eager to hear from Professor Humphreys regarding DHS's efforts since his last appearance before the subcommittee to respond to the security vulnerabilities associated with drones.

I am also looking forward to hearing from Mr. Roggero, who will be able to better inform this subcommittee about emerging technology that can be used to increase the safety of our airspace and our security posture as drones become increasingly integrated into our National airspace. Last, I am pleased that Chief Beary, the president of the International Association of Chiefs of Police, is appearing before this subcommittee.

Although you are here today to testify about the use of drones in law enforcement, I cannot forego the opportunity to talk with you about an issue that is very important to me and my constituents—that is the recent report from the Department of Justice on policing in Ferguson, Missouri, which found that many predominantly African-American neighborhoods are targeted in an effort to raise revenue for financial functions.

My question will be: Are drones possibly—can they possibly be mechanisms used for accountability, such as body cameras will be? I want to thank you for the fine job that you are doing, but this issue really must be addressed.

Now, back to the specifics of drones. Commercially-available drones are becoming an increasingly popular purchase, with the drone market expected to grow $84 billion over the next 5 years. As the commercial drone market grows, so, too, does the threat that drones will be used by actors with ill intent.

Drones can be purchased on-line with prices starting as low as $40, and they are fairly easy to assemble and learn how to operate. In many cases, it is easier to learn how to operate a drone than it is a model aircraft.

With drones being so easily accessible, we must consider the potential they have to be used as mechanisms to conduct an attack.

Although we have not yet witnessed such an attack, we have seen how individuals operating drones have gotten extraordinarily close to at least one head of state. During the campaign rallying in 2013, the drone, piloted by an opposition party supporter, landed at the feet of the chancellor of Germany, Angela Merkel, as mentioned by my Chairman.

There have also been recent stories of mysterious drones flying over sensitive Government assets, including the U.S. Embassy in Paris, and we are all familiar with the story regarding the drone landing on the White House lawn in January. It does not take wild imagination to envision what may happen if someone with malicious intent got their hands on drones.

This emerging threat requires a unified effort by the Department of Homeland Security in developing security plans for mitigation and response. The Department of Homeland Security must conduct risk assessment to accurately determine the threat posed by drones.

In the absence of risk assessments and a measured approach, the Department will spend millions of dollars without knowing what the real threat is or how to defend against it.

Unfortunately, the Department of Homeland Security declined this invitation to testify before this subcommittee to explain how they are working toward a Department-wide strategy and address the issues at hand. Even without the Department's testimony, I am confident that the panel of witnesses that are here today will help us better understand the threat posed by drones and the technologies available to address that threat.

Although drones are not the only avenue for conducting attacks, it is imperative that we leave the bad guys with fewer rather than a whole universe of options. We will narrow the threat picture by dealing with the security vulnerabilities posed by commercially-available drones while still recognizing the economic benefits of the industry.

With that, Mr. Chairman, I thank you and I yield back the balance of my time.

[The statement of Ranking Member Watson Coleman follows:]

STATEMENT OF RANKING MEMBER BONNIE WATSON COLEMAN

MARCH 18, 2015

I am very interested in hearing from Professor McNeal, an expert on the issue of drones, about the potential policy options available to mitigate and respond to the threats posed by the commercial availability of Unmanned Aerial Systems.

Additionally, I am eager to hear from Professor Humphreys regarding DHS' efforts, since his last appearance before the subcommittee, to respond to the security vulnerabilities associated with drones.

I am also looking forward to hearing from Mr. Roggero who will be able to better inform the subcommittee about emerging technology that can be used to increase the safety of our airspace and our security posture as drones become increasingly integrated into our National airspace.

Lastly, I am pleased that Chief Beary, the president of the International Association of Chiefs of Police, is appearing before the subcommittee.

Although you are here to testify about the use of drones in law enforcement, I cannot forgo the opportunity to talk with you about an issue that is very important to me and my constituents.

That is, the recent report from the Department of Justice on policing in Ferguson, Missouri, which found that many predominantly African American neighborhoods are targeted in an effort to raise revenue for municipal functions. I want to thank you for the fine job you are doing, but this issue must be addressed.

Now, back to the subject of drones. Commercially-available drones are becoming an increasingly popular purchase, with the drone market expected to grow $84 billion over the next 5 years.

As the commercial drone market grows, so too does the threat that drones will be used by actors with ill intent. Drones can be purchased on-line, with prices starting as low as $40, and they are fairly easy to assemble and learn how to operate. In many cases, it is easier to learn how to operate a drone than it is a model aircraft.

With drones being so easily accessible, we must consider the potential they have to be used as a mechanism to conduct an attack. Although we have not yet witnessed such an attack, we have seen how individuals operating drones have gotten extraordinarily close to at least one Head of State.

During a campaign rally in 2013, a drone, piloted by an opposition party supporter landed at the feet of Germany's Chancellor, Angela Merkel. There have also been recent stories of mysterious drones flying over sensitive Government assets, including the U.S. Embassy, in Paris and we are all familiar with the story regarding a drone landing on the White House lawn in January.

It does not take a wild imagination to envision what may happen if someone with malicious intent got their hands on a drone. This emerging threat requires a unified effort by the Department of Homeland Security in developing security plans for mitigation and response.

The Department of Homeland Security must conduct risk assessments to accurately determine the threat posed by drones.

In the absence of risk assessments and a measured approach, the Department will spend millions of dollars without knowing what the real threat is or how to defend against it.

Unfortunately, the Department of Homeland Security declined our invitation to testify before the subcommittee to explain how they are working towards a Department-wide strategy to address the issue at hand. Even without the Department's testimony, I am confident that the panel of witnesses here today will help us better understand the threat posed by drones and the technologies available to address that threat.

Although drones are not the only avenue for conducting attacks, it is imperative that we leave the "bad guys" with fewer, rather than a whole universe of options.

We will narrow the threat picture by dealing with the security vulnerabilities posed by commercially-available drones.

Mr. PERRY. Chairman thanks the gentlelady.

The Chairman now recognizes the Ranking Member of the full committee, the gentleman from Mississippi, Mr. Thompson.

Mr. THOMPSON. Thank you, Mr. Chairman, and thank you for holding this important and timely hearing.

On a daily basis articles are published about the suspicious use of commercially-available drones. In recent weeks drones have been observed flying over sensitive locations in Paris. According to French authorities, drones have flown over nuclear installations, the home of the French president, and the United States Embassy.

Here in the United States, a drone recently crashed on the White House grounds. While the incident at the White House has been described by officials as nothing more than a drunken misadventure, it raises questions about the threat commercially-available drones may pose to individuals, infrastructure, and our aviation systems.

Undoubtedly, drones have great potential. In Japan, drones have been used by farmers for years as an efficient and effective tool for crop fertilization. Projects for commercial use in the United States display that drones will become a common sight on farms in Pennsylvania and my home State of Mississippi in the coming years.

In the wrong hands, however, these potentially valuable commercial tools could become dangerous instruments for attack. That is why it is critical that the Department of Homeland Security conduct risk assessments to determine what steps should be taken to mitigate the potential threat.

To date, we have learned of components of the Department, such as Secret Service and the Science and Technology Directorate, conducting testing that identifies methods to address the potential threats drones pose. It is less clear whether there is a Department-wide strategy to develop—to address the issue.

Unfortunately, despite being invited, as previously commented, the Department of Homeland Security is not here today to explain why and to Members what is being done to address the security vulnerabilities drones expose. Despite the Department's absence, I am confident that the Members will receive valuable testimony from this distinguished panel of witnesses assembled.

Professor McNeal is an expert on the issues of drones and will add a valuable voice to our conversation about the policy solutions should be explored to address the security concerns surrounding drones. Professor Humphreys is making his second appearance before the subcommittee to discuss the issue. I look forward to the other witnesses' testimony also.

Finally, I am pleased that Chief Beary is appearing in his capacity as president of the International Association of Chiefs of Police. We all have questions Chief Beary can address regarding how law enforcement utilizes drones and how they respond to drone operating in our cities.

However, before yielding back, Mr. Chairman, I am compelled to point out that much of what we, and now the public, know of the Secret Service's testing of drones is the result of leaks. Unfortunately, it is all too common an occurrence that information provided to Members and staff in our security space to be published by the media in the next days and hours after the briefing.

This committee has a responsibility to the American people to make the Department of Homeland Security work and, accordingly, our Nation more secure. Leaking Classified information is in direct conflict with that responsibility. It is also in conflict with the law and the oath we signed to obtain access to Classified information.

I hope and trust all Members and staff of this committee and those of other committees we invite to attend briefings will take the oath and the responsibility that comes with it to heart.

With that, Mr. Chairman, I yield back.

[The statement of Ranking Member Thompson follows:]

STATEMENT OF RANKING MEMBER BENNIE G. THOMPSON

MARCH 18, 2015

On a daily basis, articles are published about the suspicious use of commercially-available drones. In recent weeks, drones have been observed flying over sensitive locations in Paris. According to French authorities, drones have flown over nuclear installations, the home of the French President, and near the United States embassy.

Here in the United States, a drone recently crashed on the White House grounds. While the incident at the White House has been described by officials as nothing more than a drunken misadventure, it raised questions about the threat commercially available drones may pose to individuals, infrastructure, and our aviation system.

Undoubtedly, drones have great potential. In Japan, drones have been used by farmers for years as an efficient and effective tool for crop fertilization. Projections for commercial use in the United States display that drones will become a common sight on farms from Pennsylvania to Mississippi in the coming years.

In the wrong hands, these potentially valuable commercial tools could become dangerous instruments for attack. That is why it is critical that the Department of Homeland Security conduct risk assessments to determine what steps should be taken to mitigate the potential threat.

To date, we have learned of components of the Department, such as the Secret Service and Science and Technology Directorate, conducting testing to identify methods to address the potential threat drones pose. It is less clear whether there is a Department-wide strategy being developed to address the issue.

Unfortunately, despite being invited to testify, the Department of Homeland Security is not here today to explain to Members what is being done to address the security vulnerability drones expose. Despite the Department's absence, I am confident that the Members will receive valuable testimony from the distinguished panel of witnesses assembled.

Professor McNeal is an expert on the issue of drones and will add a valuable voice to our conversation about what policy solutions should be explored to address the security concerns surrounding drones.

Professor Humphries is making his second appearance before the subcommittee to discuss this issue. I look forward to hearing from him regarding the progress DHS has made regarding drones since his appearance in 2012.

I also look forward to hearing from Mr. Roggero regarding potential technological solutions to the threat posed by drones.

Finally, I am please that Chief Beary is appearing in his capacity as president of the International Association of Chiefs of Police. We all have questions Chief Beary can address regarding how law enforcement utilizes drones and how they respond to drones operating in our cities.

Before yielding back Mr. Chairman, I am compelled to point out that much of what we, and now the public, knows about the Secret Service's testing of drones is the result of leaks. Unfortunately, it is an all too common occurrence for information provided to Members and staff in our secure space to be published by the media in the days and hours after briefings.

This committee has a responsibility to the American people to make the Department of Homeland Security work and accordingly our Nation more secure.

Leaking Classified information is in direct conflict with that responsibility. It is also in conflict with the law and oath we signed to obtain access to Classified information. I hope, and trust, all Members and staff of this committee, and those on other committees we invite to attend briefings, will take the oath and the responsibility that comes with it to heart.

Mr. PERRY. Chairman thanks the gentleman.

Other Members of the subcommittee are reminded that opening statements may be submitted for the record.

We are pleased to have a distinguished panel of witnesses before us today on this important topic.

Let me remind the witnesses that their entire written statement will appear in the record, and I will introduce each of you first and then recognize you for your testimony.

Dr. Todd Humphreys is a professor at the Cockrell School of Engineering at the University of Texas at Austin. He directs their radio navigation laboratory at U.T. Austin, where his research focuses on defending against intentional GPS spoofing and jamming.

Dr. Humphreys' research has uncovered that GPS signals that navigate unmanned aerial systems can be hijacked and controlled. Dr. Humphreys obtained his doctorate from Cornell University.

Mr. Frederick Roggero is president—got that correct, don't I, General—president and CEO of Resilient Solutions. Mr. Roggero is an expert in commercial unmanned aerial systems.

Previously, Mr. Roggero served as the chief of safety of the U.S. Air Force, where he oversaw all Air Force aviation, ground, weapons, space, and systems mishap prevention, and nuclear surety programs. Mr. Roggero is also a pilot with over 4,000 hours in 22 different type of military aircraft. Mr. Roggero retired from the Air Force with the rank of major general.

Thank you for your service, sir.

Chief Richard Beary is president of the International Association of Chiefs of Police. Chief Beary served for over 30 years as a law enforcement officer in Florida, including as chief of police for the University of Central Florida, the largest university in the State. Chief Beary was awarded the Medal of Valor twice in his career.

Thank you for your service, sir.

Dr. Gregory McNeal is a professor at Pepperdine University, where his research and teaching focus is on National security law and policy, criminal law and procedure, and international law. Previously he served as assistant director of the Institute for Global Security and codirected a transnational counterterrorism grant program at the U.S. Justice Department. Dr. McNeal obtained his doctorate from Pennsylvania State University.

Go Lions.

All right. Thank you all for being here today.

Chairman now recognizes Dr. Humphreys for his testimony.

STATEMENT OF TODD E. HUMPHREYS, ASSISTANT PRO-FESSOR, COCKRELL SCHOOL OF ENGINEERING, THE UNI-VERSITY OF TEXAS AT AUSTIN

Mr. HUMPHREYS. Chairman Perry, Ranking Member Watson Coleman, and Ranking Member Thompson, last August the U.T. football season opener was interrupted by a drone. There were nearly 100,000 football fans in the stadium that day and the police had to stand by watching helplessly as this drone shifted around the stadium.

The incident only ended when the operator decided to recall the drone and it landed at his feet.

The situation turned out to be harmless. This was just a case of a ticketless but devoted U.T. football fan who just wanted to watch the game. But the police couldn't have known that before-hand, so they had to treat the incident as a potential attack on the multitude of gathered spectators.

In the years to come, this intrusion at the U.T. football stadium will be replayed in various forms at sites critical to the security of the United States. The great majority of these incidents will be accidently, like the flyaway drone that crashed at the White House in January.

But in the early stages of a drone incursion, it is impossible to distinguish the accidental from the intentional, the malignant from the benign. The distressing truth is that even consumer-grade drones can be rigged to carry out potent attacks, and against these attacks our defenses will either be only weakly effective or so militarized as to pose themselves a threat to bystanders and the surrounding civil infrastructure.

In thinking about how to detect and defend against rogue UAVs, it is useful to distinguish three categories. First are the accidental intrusions; second are the intentional intrusions by unsophisticated operators; and third are the intentional intrusions by sophisticated operators—these are people who know how to modify the hardware and software of a drone to make it do what they want.

Detecting and safely repelling intrusions of the first two categories is not simple, but it is quite possible. Commercial UAV manufacturers can play a key role here by implementing GPS-enforced geo-fences within their autopilot systems. That simple fix would prevent accidental and unsophisticated drone intrusions into restricted airspace.

So what about the third type—the sophisticated malicious attacks? These will be much more difficult to counter. The fact is that for any reasonable defense I can imagine, I can also imagine a counter to that defense, a way to circumvent that defense.

I am not alone. Any one of my graduate students at the University of Texas, or many undergraduate students walking the halls of universities across the globe, or those part of the do-it-yourself community, hobbyists—these people have the kind of skills that would be required to carry out one of the sophisticated attacks I mentioned. The documentation is also extensive.

So what should we do? Well, let's start with what we shouldn't do.

It won't help to impose stricter regulations on small UAS than the sensible regulations the FAA has already proposed. Likewise, restricting open-source autopilot platforms would hardly improve security, but it would stifle innovation. Military-style radio link or GPS jamming or spoofing wouldn't stop a sophisticated attacker, but would endanger commercial airliners and disrupt communications.

In my view, the most sensible way forward is to focus on accidental and unsophisticated UAV intrusions. Let's encourage the UAV manufacturers to put geo-fences in their autopilot systems.

For especially sensitive sites like the White House, we could deploy a network of infrared cameras set up to detect and track an incoming drone by looking for the thermal signatures of its warm batteries and motors. This network of sensors could be used to guide an always-ready squadron of interceptor drones that could capture the intruder in a net can carry it off.

But we should refrain from any more drastic measures than these until the threat of UAVs proves to be more of a menace than the recent incidents, which, while alarming, were ultimately harmless.

Thank you.

[The prepared statement of Dr. Humphreys follows:]

PREPARED STATEMENT OF TODD HUMPHREYS

MARCH 16, 2015

1. SUMMARY

The nearly 100,000 football fans gathered in Texas Memorial Stadium last August to watch the Longhorn football season opener had trouble concentrating on the game. Hovering above the stadium was an unmanned aerial vehicle (UAV), a drone, with blue and red blinking lights. The University of Texas Police watched helplessly as the UAV shifted from one area of the stadium to another. When the UAV's operator finally recalled the device and landed it at his feet in a nearby parking lot, the police immediately took both UAV and operator into custody.

The situation turned out to be no more menacing than a devoted but ticketless UT football fan trying to watch the game through the video feed on his drone. But the police could not have known this before-hand, and so had to treat the incident as a potential chemical, biological, or explosive attack on the multitude of gathered spectators.

As we enter an age of highly capable and increasingly autonomous UAVs purchasable for a few hundred dollars over the internet, the intrusion at the UT football stadium will be replayed in various forms at sites critical to the security of the United States. The great majority of these incidents will be accidental, such as the flyaway UAV that crashed on the White House grounds in January. But in the early stages of a UAV incursion, it will be impossible to distinguish the accidental from the intentional, the benign from the malicious. And the distressing truth is that even consumer-grade UAVs can be rigged to carry out potent attacks against which our defenses will either be only weakly effective or so militarized that the defenses themselves will pose a threat to the surrounding civil infrastructure.

UAVs have been around for a long time. The Academy of Model Aeronautics was founded in 1936 and since that time a vibrant and knowledgeable community of radio-controlled model aircraft enthusiasts has been active in the United States and across the globe. What explains, then, the recent uptick in alarming UAV sightings near sensitive sites? The answer is clear: Never before have highly-capable UAVs been so inexpensive and widely available. One can buy over the internet today a UAV that rivals the increasingly autonomous surveillance and guidance capability of military UAVs. Many of these commercial UAVs can easily carry a payload of a couple of pounds or more.

In thinking about how to detect and defend against UAV incursions into sensitive airspace, it is useful to distinguish three categories. First are the accidental intrusions, whether the UAV operators are sophisticated or not. Second are intentional intrusions by unsophisticated operators. Third are intentional intrusions by sophisticated operators—those capable of assembling a UAV from components and modifying its hardware and software.

Detecting and safely repelling intrusions of the first two types is not simple but is quite possible. Commercial UAV manufacturers can play a key role here by implementing GPS-enforced geofences within their autopilot systems that prevent their UAVs from being flown within exclusion zones around airports, sports stadiums, Government buildings, and other security-sensitive sites. The sites themselves could be equipped with radar, acoustic, and electro-optical sensors for UAV detection, and with powerful and agile interceptor UAVs, possibly working as a team, that could capture and carry off a small number of simultaneous intruders.

UAV intrusions of the third type will be much more difficult to counter. A sophisticated attacker could mount a kamikaze-style attack against a sensitive target using a fixed-wing powered glider with an explosive few-pound payload. The UAV glider could be launched tens of miles from the target.

It could cut its engine on final approach to evade acoustic detectors, and could be built of poorly-radar-reflective material (e.g., Styrofoam) to evade radar detection. With only minor changes to the UAV's autopilot software, of which highly-capable open-source variants exist, an attacker could readily disable geofencing and could configure the UAV to operate under "radio silence," ignoring external radio control commands and emitting no radio signals of its own. The UAV would thus be difficult to detect and would be impervious to command link jamming or hijacking. Moreover, the attacker could configure the autopilot to ignore GPS/GNSS signals during the final approach to the target, relying instead on an inexpensive magnetometer-disciplined inertial navigation system. Such a modification would render GPS/GNSS jamming or deception (spoofing) useless during final approach.

It is not obvious how to protect critical civil infrastructure against such a UAV, or—worse yet—against a swarm of such UAVs. What is more, the skills required of operators in this third category are not uncommon: The do-it-yourself UAV and autopilot development communities are large and the documentation of both hardware and software is extensive. One should also bear in mind that the threshold for a successful attack is low when success is measured by the ability to cause widespread panic or economic disruption. For example, explosion of a UAV anywhere on the White House grounds could be seen as a highly successful attack even if it causes only minor physical damage.

What can be done? First, it is important to take stock of what should not be done. Imposing restrictions on small UAVs beyond the sensible restrictions the Federal Aviation Administration recently proposed would not significantly reduce the threat of rogue UAVs yet would shackle the emerging commercial UAV industry. In fact, even the FAA's current ban on non-line-of-sight UAV control would be of little consequence to a malefactor capable of modifying an open-source autopilot. Likewise, restricting open-source autopilot platforms would hardly improve security but would stifle innovation. Powerful and persistent wide-area GPS/GNSS jamming would prevent inexpensive UAV attacks launched from miles away from reaching their targets, but this military-style defense would be disruptive to civil use of GPS over a wide area. Powerful GPS jamming around the White House, for example, would deny GPS aiding to commercial aircraft at nearby Reagan National Airport. Similarly, anti-UAV laser or electromagnetic pulse systems are a danger to nearby civil infrastructure and transport.

From a strictly technological point of view, the best way forward will be to adopt simple measures that sharply reduce the risk of category 1 and 2 incidents, such as voluntary manufacturer-imposed geofencing. For especially critical sites, detection and tracking systems based on electro-optical sensors will be most effective, particularly those applying infrared sensor pattern recognition to distinguish a UAV's warm motors and batteries from a bird's warm body. The output of such a detection and tracking system could be fed to an always-ready squadron of interceptor UAVs whose job would be to catch the intruder in a net and expel it, or, as a last resort, to collide with it and force it down. We should refrain from any more drastic measures than this until the threat of UAVs proves to be more of a menace than the recent incidents, which were alarming but harmless.

The following sections offer more detailed analysis of potential techniques for detecting, tracking, and repelling UAVs.

2. DETECTION AND TRACKING

This section gives an overview of techniques that may be used to detect and track UAVs operating in restricted airspace. Merits and drawbacks of each technique are noted.

2.1 *Conventional Surveillance: Radar and Beacon Transmitters.*—Conventional aircraft surveillance techniques are based on radar and beacon transmissions from aircraft. The latter either respond to ground interrogation (as with secondary surveillance radar) or are broadcast from the aircraft without interrogation (as with ADS–B)[1], Ch. 5).

2.1.1 *Advantages*

    1. Primary surveillance radar (PSR) and secondary surveillance radar (SSR) systems are already installed at major airports across the United States.

    2. PSR does not assume any cooperation from the target and so is well-suited for detecting malicious intruders.

    3. If an incoming UAV is broadcasting ADS–B squitters, detecting and tracking it would be trivial.

2.1.2 *Drawbacks*

    1. UAVs do not typically carry SSR beacons, and it would be wishful thinking to expect Category 3 UAV intruders to be equipped with functioning ADS–B beacons.

    2. UAVs whose structure is made of poorly-radar-reflective materials (e.g., a fixed-wing glider made of Styrofoam) and having a wingspan less than a few meters would not be visible to PSR or would be hardly distinguishable from birds or bats. Moreover, UAVs flying at an altitude of less than 100 feet would be difficult to detect by PSR.

2.2 *Acoustic Sensing.*—The motors of electric-powered rotorcraft and fixed-wing UAVs emit a characteristic whine that can be used to detect such UAVs. Gas-powered UAVs also exhibit a characteristic acoustic signature.

2.2.1 *Advantages*

    1. Low cost, even when implemented as a network of sensing devices placed around the protection perimeter.

    2. Can be highly effective when combined with electro-optical sensing to distinguish UAVs from electric weed whackers.

    3. Forces a UAV wishing to evade detection to execute final approach as a glider or a free-falling rotorcraft.

2.2.2 *Drawbacks*

    1. Leads to false positives due to electric weed whackers or spoofing via playback of an audio recording of a UAV if not combined with other sensing modalities such as electro-optical sensing.

    2. Incapable of detecting fixed-wing UAVs operating as gliders or rotorcraft UAVs in free fall.

    3. Unlikely to offer reliable detection at more than a 500-meter standoff range.

2.3 *Radio Emission Sensing.*—UAVs typically send data back to their controller through a wireless data link. Using a directional antenna or a network of synchronized ground stations, such emissions can be detected and located.[2]

2.3.1 *Advantages*

    1. Can offer effective detection and accurate tracking of multiple UAVs with arbitrary emitted waveforms if the UAV emissions are sufficiently persistent and powerful.

2.3.2 *Drawbacks*

    1. To be economical and offer rapid detection, the system must have some knowledge of the emission center frequency and bandwidth.

    2. Easily evaded by a UAV operating under radio silence, which would be trivial for a Category 3 attacker to implement.

2.4 *Electro-Optical Sensing.*—Electro-optical (EO) sensors in the form of cameras that are sensitive to visible light or infrared radiation can be quite effective at detecting and tracking UAVs.

2.4.1 *Advantages*

    1. An EO sensing network can be built from small, low-cost sensors with only mild synchronization requirements. The network could be geographically large (e.g., it could cover the area around the White House and the U.S. Capitol in Washington, DC), which would increase the chance of detecting and the accuracy of tracking an overflying UAV.

    2. Infrared EO sensors can detect the warm motors or batteries of UAVs day or night and, with proper pattern recognition, would likely be reliable in distinguishing UAVs from birds, bats, and insects.

---

[1] K. Wesson, *Secure Navigation And Timing Without Local Storage Of Secret Keys*. PhD thesis, The University of Texas at Austin, May 2014.

[2] J.A. Bhatti, T.E. Humphreys, and B.M. Ledvina, ''Development and demonstration of a TDOA-based GNSS interference signal localization system,'' in *Proceedings of the IEEE/ION PLANS Meeting*, pp. 1209–1220, April 2012.

13

3. A network of EO sensors can offer full three-dimensional target tracking.

2.4.2 *Drawbacks*

　　1. The author is not aware of a commercial networked EO system that can provide 3-D UAV tracking and distinguish UAVs from wildlife. But there do not appear to be any serious technological roadblocks that would prevent such a system from being developed and deployed.

　　2. It is unclear what the effective range of an infrared sensor network could be. This will depend on the strength of thermal emissions from a UAV and on the pattern recognition algorithm tasked with distinguishing the UAV from wildlife.

3. ELECTRONIC DEFENSES

For typical operation, UAVs capable of autonomous flight rely on two vital wireless links: The command link to the operator and the (passive) navigation signal link to overhead GPS/GNSS spacecraft.[3] In the event of a UAV attack, a defender can attempt to disrupt these links or feed false signals to the UAV's radios.[4]

3.1 *Command Link Jamming and Appropriation.*—Modern commercial UAVs are controlled by one or more wireless links to the operator's control equipment. Traditional RC controllers are still used as a back-up means of control even for UAVs capable of a high degree of autonomy. These controllers send low-level commands to the autopilot system or directly to the UAV motors or to the servos that actuate the aircraft's control surfaces. These transmitters typically operate in unlicensed bands (often 2.4GHz), but do not typically use WiFi/802.11 protocols, preferring direct-sequence spread spectrum (DSSS) or frequency-hopped spread spectrum (FHSS) protocols that offer a large number of independent channels.

For control at a higher level of abstraction, a control station may communicate with a UAV independent of the RC controller. Like the RC controller, this link is often established within unlicensed bands. For example, the popular DJI drone establishes this link in the 2.4 GHz band using a standard WiFi/802.11 protocol. This link facilitates video downlinking and general control functionality such as parameter setting and high-level trajectory control.

In defending a sensitive site from UAV intrusion, a defender may attempt to jam or appropriate the command link.

3.1.1 *Advantages*

　　1. Command link jamming or appropriation is an effective means of denying a hostile operator the ability to execute an RC-controlled visual line-of-sight UAV attack or a first-person-viewer (FPV) UAV attack.

　　2. Command link jamming forces an attacking UAV to operate independently from its human operators.

　　3. Command link appropriation can enable a defender to obtain full control of an intruder UAV.

3.1.2 *Drawbacks*

　　1. Although the signals from today's commercially-available RC controllers are not encrypted or authenticated, the UAV is paired with the RC controller in such a way that the two agree on a communications channel selected from a large number (e.g., 100) of possible channels. Thus, to appropriate the RC link, a defender would need to determine at least: (1) Which communications protocol is being used (e.g., DSSS or FHSS), (2) which channel within the protocol is being used.

　　2. Although the command and data link to the control station is not typically encrypted or authenticated, it can be encrypted with well-established cryptographic algorithms using openly available software*, rendering appropriation of this link difficult at best.

　　3. To avoid the effects of command link jamming or appropriation, an attacking UAV can simply transition to an autonomous operational mode soon after take-off, accepting no further external commands.

3.2 *GPS/GNSS Interference.*—Virtually all modern commercial UAVs capable of autonomous flight exploit navigation signals from overhead GPS satellites. The UAV's satellite navigation receiver may also be capable of exploiting signals from other Global Navigation Satellite Systems (GNSS) such as the European Galileo system and the Russian GLONASS system. It is well-known that civil GNSS signals are

---

[3] K.D. Wesson and T.E. Humphreys, "Hacking drones," *Scientific American*, vol. 309, no. 5, pp. 54–59, 2013.

[4] A.J. Kerns, D.P. Shepard, J.A. Bhatti, and T.E. Humphreys, "Unmanned aircraft capture and control via GPS spoofing," *Journal of Field Robotics*, vol. 31, no. 4, pp. 617–636, 2014.

* See, for example, *http://phantommods.info/effect-on-wifi-encryption-for-fpv-range/*.

weak and, to date, unencrypted and unauthenticated,[5] although proposals exist to insert digital signatures into the broadcast GPS and Galileo navigation data streams.[6][7][8] In the face of a deliberate UAV attack guided by GNSS signals, a defender could take advantage of the weak security of GNSS signals to confuse or commandeer the attacking UAV.

3.2.1 *Advantages*

1. Three-dimensional hostile control of a UAV via GPS deception (spoofing) is possible: It has been demonstrated in the laboratory and in a Government-supervised experiment at White Sands Missile Test Range.[4]

2. Even if the location of an incoming UAV is known only very approximately (e.g., it is only known that a UAV is approaching the White House grounds from the southwest), GPS deception can be effective at repelling an attack. If one sectorizes the area around the site to be protected into 4 quadrants, each quadrant covered by a directional transmission antenna, then a UAV approaching under GPS guidance, or a group of UAVs, can be made to believe it has overshot its target, causing the UAV to slow and eventually proceed away from the target site as if facing a stiff headwind. The University of Texas Radionavigation Laboratory recently demonstrated this defense in the laboratory against the GPS receiver used in a large number of commercial UAVs.

3. Persistent and powerful GNSS jamming would force attackers to operate either by: (1) Line-of-sight (LOS) RC control, (2) first-person viewer (FPV) control, or (3) non-GNSS autonomous navigation. LOS control exposes the operator to visual detection and recognition. LOS and FPV control can be denied by control link jamming. And non-GNSS autonomous navigation in an unmapped environment is either expensive (e.g., a navigation- or tactical-grade INS initialized with GNSS), can only be applied accurately over short time intervals (e.g., a MEMS-grade magnetometer-disciplined INS),[9] or still in the research stage (e.g., autonomous visual navigation).[10]

3.2.2 *Drawbacks*

1. Persistent and powerful GNSS jamming would cause substantial collateral damage, denying the use of civil GNSS in a wide area around the protected site, which possibly encompasses airports.[5] Powerful GPS jamming around the White House, for example, would deny GPS aiding to commercial aircraft at nearby Reagan National Airport. Such jamming would alter civil operational procedures in the area: Automobile commuters would be denied use of their in-car navigation systems, cell towers could no longer be synchronized by GPS, and approaches to airports could no longer benefit from GPS for safety and efficiency. While it is not out of the question to engage in powerful GNSS jamming to protect extremely sensitive sites such as the White House, it is the opinion of the author that this would need to be a last resort. It would need to be carefully coordinated with the DOT and DHS.

2. Even intermittent GNSS jamming powerful enough to deny UAV use of GNSS would be problematic for the surrounding civil infrastructure. UAV GNSS receivers are typically high-sensitivity receivers capable of operating at carrier-to-noise ratios (CNRs) as low as 15 dB-Hz (e.g.,[11]). By contrast, the GPS receivers used in commercial aviation typically fail to track signals below a CNR of 29 dB-Hz. Therefore, to effectively jam a UAV located 1 km from the White House would require a jamming power that would also effectively deny

---

[5] T.E. Humphreys, "Statement on the vulnerability of civil unmanned aerial vehicles and other systems to civil GPS spoofing." *http://homeland.house.gov/sites/homeland.house.gov/files/Testimony-Humphreys.pdf*, July 2012.

[6] K.D. Wesson, M.P. Rothlisberger, and T.E. Humphreys, "Practical cryptographic civil GPS signal authentication," Navigation, *Journal of the Institute of Navigation*, vol. 59, no. 3, pp. 177–193, 2012.

[7] A.J. Kerns, K.D. Wesson, and T.E. Humphreys, "A blueprint for civil GPS navigation message authentication," in *Proceedings of the IEEE/ION PLANS Meeting*, May 2014.

[8] I.F. Hernandez, V. Rijmen, G.S. Granados, J. Simon, I. Rodriguez, and J.D. Calle, "Design drivers, solutions and robustness assessment of navigation message authentication for the Galileo open service," in *Proceedings of the ION GNSS+ Meeting*, 2014.

[9] O. Woodman, "An introduction to inertial navigation," *University of Cambridge, Computer Laboratory, Tech. Rep. UCAMCL–TR–696*, 2007.

[10] G. Chowdhary, E.N. Johnson, D. Magree, A. Wu, and A. Shein, "GPS-denied indoor and outdoor monocular vision aided navigation and control of unmanned aircraft," *Journal of Field Robotics*, vol. 30, no. 3, pp. 415–437, 2013.

[5] T.E. Humphreys, "Statement on the vulnerability of civil unmanned aerial vehicles and other systems to civil GPS spoofing." *http://homeland.house.gov/sites/homeland.house.gov/files/Testimony-Humphreys.pdf*, July 2012.

[11] u-Blox, *Datasheet: NE0–6 GPS Module.*

GNSS to a commercial aircraft along the same line of sight more than 5 km from the White House.

3. GNSS spoofing would potentially be even more damaging to surrounding civil systems than GNSS jamming, and thus would need to be carefully coordinated with the DOT and DHS. Moreover, to be absolutely reliable, a GNSS spoofer would have to create simulated signals for all available civil GNSS, including Galileo and GLONASS.

4. An attacking UAV can simply disregard GNSS signals during the final approach to the target, relying, for example, on a low-cost magnetometer-disciplined MEMS-grade inertial navigation system, which, over a 60-second interval, may only exhibit a 5-meter drift in perceived location.[9]

4. KINETIC DEFENSES

Kinetic defenses encompass all techniques that involve mechanical contact with the UAV intruder such as interceptor UAVs, rubber bullets, shotgun shot, or nets.

4.1.3 *Advantages*

1. Net capture of UAVs by interceptor UAVs has been demonstrated (though it cannot yet be considered a mature technology). Net capture has the additional benefit of enabling eviction of the intruder UAV from the vicinity of the site to be protected.

2. Commercial UAVs are, in general, fragile in the face of kinetic attacks.

4.1.4 *Drawbacks*

1. All kinetic defenses require reliable detection and accurate tracking of the UAV intruder.

2. Hard-contact kinetic defenses such as collision with an interceptor UAV may cause an intruder UAV carrying an explosive payload to explode.

3. Interceptor UAV technology is currently immature.

5. ACKNOWLEDGMENTS

The author is grateful to Mark Psiaki, Christopher Hegarty, Andrew Kerns, Nathan Green, Michael Szmuk, and Daniel Shepard for insightful conversations on how to protect critical civil sites from UAV intrusion.

Mr. PERRY. Chairman thanks Dr. Humphreys.

Chairman now recognizes Mr. Roggero for his testimony.

STATEMENT OF MAJOR GENERAL FREDERICK F. ROGGERO, (USAF–RET.), PRESIDENT AND CHIEF EXECUTIVE OFFICER, RESILIENT SOLUTIONS, LTD.

General ROGERRO. Thank you very much, Mr. Chairman, and thank you for the opportunity to appear before you today, Ranking Member Watson Coleman and Ranking Member Thompson, ladies and gentlemen.

Aviation is undergoing a global revolution as we sit here today. With advances in unmanned technologies that are moving ahead at the speed of Moore's Law, as you have indicated already, while associated prices are continue to fall, small, unmanned aerial systems have become high-tech and universally available tools.

Coupled with advances in autopilots, telemetry, sensor and camera miniaturization, small UASs are delivering capabilities that were once only the purview of nation states. Now almost anyone can experience the advantages of thrills of aviation without ever having to leave the ground, taking a flight physical, or getting a check ride.

As these barriers to entry continue to fall, we are witnessing the democratization of aviation.

These new technologies give individuals a limited version of the unique characteristics of aviation—speed, range, flexibility, and al-

[9] O. Woodman, "An introduction to inertial navigation," *University of Cambridge, Computer Laboratory, Tech. Rep. UCAMCL–TR–696*, 2007.

titude—that are enjoyed by every air force in the world. It is true that small UASs are capable of making our lives better by helping us to imagine more, safer ways to do our jobs that are dangerous, dull, and dirty. But they are also a terrific means to enhance commerce, save lives, gain different perspectives, and even to provide recreation.

But as with all revolutions, there are risks that must be dealt with, and the safety and security risks of small drones are no exception. However, as the risk of these types of aircraft are reviewed, we must strive to preserve and to protect the overwhelming benefits that this rapidly-expanding technology will bring for generations to come.

The risks inherent in this revolution can be divided into two parts: Safety and security. Safety because we have a growing class of new operators who don't understand that they have just become part of the aviation system and are flying a piece of equipment that is capable of operating in the same space as an airliner. But this type of safety risk can and should be dealt with through a public campaign of education, regulation, and enforcement.

Next are those small UAS operators that know the rules but decide to violate them anyway. It is operators from this class that will most likely cause the first collision between an aircraft and a drone in the United States. But once again, public awareness; standard, clear regulations; firm penalties; and enforcement are the best remedies to slow these types of transgressions.

At this point we move into the security risks. Tasks such as intelligence gathering, surveillance, reconnaissance, attack, and mobility can all be conducted with easily available UASs at very reasonable prices. These actions could be directed at National critical infrastructure points, factories, VIPs, and other examples, as we have heard this morning.

Much work has already been done in this area of defense by our NATO partners, and we should take advantage of those developed solutions and lessons learned. For example, the United Kingdom took this threat so seriously in 2012 that the Royal Air Force and Selex ES designed and deployed an integrated counter-small UAS system in London to defend the Olympic Stadium during the opening ceremonies. This system was further improved and used to defend world leaders during the 2013 G8 Summit in Ireland.

Certainly the lessons learned from these efforts could inform our actions as we address these common threats.

I believe that our way should be a simultaneous two-prong solution. First, use commercial, off-the-shelf technology that has already been developed, tested, refined, and used operationally in this role to establish a baseline capability for us immediately. By using a layered defense, the threat can be neutralized and the physical and electronic forensic evidence be preserved for arrest and prosecution.

We should pick what works best for our needs, and I will refer you to my submitted statement for a listing of the elements that I believe are required for a multiple-layered, integrated UAS defense.

The second simultaneous track starts with interagency cooperation to draft an overarching strategy and linked policies that have a legal and regulatory basis to deal with unmanned systems in general, and unmanned aerial systems in particular.

Ranking Member Thompson, I would say that this strategy needs to be Government-wide and not just focused on DHS.

This is where the departments and agencies will need to help to ensure that they have the legal framework necessary to respond to this threat.

Furthermore, a single department should be nominated as the executive agent, and provided with the right resources and charged with leading this effort across the Government.

In summary, my written statement provides several recommendations for consideration by the committee to tackle this problem, and by capitalizing on best practices and technology already applied by our international allies such as the United Kingdom, we could be ready to deal with today's threats immediately while we draft the correct policies and spin up U.S. industries, universities, and laboratories to rapidly explore ways to counter tomorrow's drones and the unique threats that they will bring in the next 2 to 5 years.

Thank you very much.

[The prepared statement of General Roggero follows:]

PREPARED STATEMENT OF FREDERICK F. ROGGERO

MARCH 18, 2015

THE CURRENT ENVIRONMENT

Aviation is undergoing a global revolution. With advances in unmanned system technology that are moving at the speed of "Moore's Law," while their associated prices continue to fall, "Class 1" small, unmanned aerial systems (sUAS) have become high-tech, universally available tools. Coupled with advances in autopilots, telemetry, sensor and camera miniaturization, and corresponding increases in battery and engine capacities, sUAS's are delivering capabilities that were once only the purview of nation-states, corporations, and wealthy individuals. Now, almost anyone can experience the advantages and thrills of aviation without ever leaving the ground, taking a flight physical, spending hours and considerable funds to hone a skill, or complete a rigorous training and certification process. As these barriers-to-entry continue to fall, we will witness the democratization of aviation.

This combination of new, expanding, technologies delivers a limited version of the unique characteristics of aviation (speed, range, flexibility, and altitude) enjoyed by every air force directly to individuals and groups around the globe. And, as drone technologies improve, airpower concepts such as "stealth" and "air supremacy" could even become available to more common operators. It's true that sUAS's are capable of making our lives better by helping us to imagine new, more safe, ways to do jobs that are dangerous, dull, and dirty. They are also a terrific means to enhance commerce, save lives, gain different perspectives, and even to provide recreation. But, as with all revolutions, there are risks that must be dealt with. And, the safety and security risks of small drones are no exemption. However, as the risk of these types of aircraft are reviewed, we must also strive to preserve and protect the overwhelming benefits that this rapidly expanding technology will bring for generations to come.

The risk inherent in the drone revolution can be divided into two sections—safety and security. Although the Academy of Model Aeronautics does a terrific job of providing voluntary safety standards, the exploding growth of this market means that many new recreational users of small drones simply do not understand that there is an aviation culture of safety. The days of the remote-control flying field with noisy gas motors and plenty of mentors is disappearing. The new group of "park flyers" haven't received education or training in safety, airspace, weather, air traffic control, emergency procedures, or even basic airmanship. Because of that, a few in this segment will eventually pose a safety hazard by unknowingly flying in areas that they are not allowed to operate, not out of malice, but because they simply do not understand the rules. But this type of safety risk can, and should, be dealt with through education, regulation, and enforcement.

Next on the ladder of safety risk are those drone operators that know the rules but decided to violate them. Perhaps they feel the need to test out the new technology, to see how high, fast, or far it can go, or to obtain video from perspectives not allowed, usually for good reason. It is operators from this class that will most likely cause the first collision between an aircraft and a drone in the United States. But, once again, standard, clear regulation and enforcement are the best remedies for these types of transgressions.

At this point, we move into the risks to our security. This revolutionary technology can be an affordable asymmetric tool for those who want to use its capabilities for illegitimate purposes. For less than $1,000 one could purchase a system that would allow you to conduct traditional "air force" missions, at limited, but still effective, levels of success. Tasks such as intelligence gathering, surveillance, reconnaissance, attack, and mobility can all be conducted with commercially-available systems. These actions could be directed at National critical infrastructure points, factories, VIPs, military bases, prisons, large public gatherings, the borders, or simply, a neighborhood.

THE CHALLENGE

The U.S. Government must be able to protect its sensitive critical infrastructure, personnel, and citizens from the malicious use of small drones, while preserving the best aspects of using small sUAS's commercially and recreationally. There will be a balancing act as we deter, mitigate, and defeat these types of security threats while preserving the benefits that sUAS's bring. Much work has already been done in this area by our international partners and allies and we should take advantage of those developed solutions and "lessons learned."

THE THREAT

Small UAS's are easy to make, cheap to buy, simple to fly, hard to detect, carry small versatile payloads, have a disruptive capability, and are evolving and proliferating quickly. "Lone Wolves," activists, thieves, terrorist groups, etc. could use this reliable and inexpensive capability to conduct intelligence gathering or execute missions against a variety of targets using explosives, chemicals, powder, etc. to deliver a disruptive attack via a single aircraft, or through more sophisticated coordinated, or multi-platform, attacks. Since 2013 smugglers have already tried to use the mobility capability of sUAS's to deliver 6.6 lbs. of crystal meth across the Mexico-U.S. border and to deliver tobacco and cell phones into a prison in Georgia and marijuana into a South Carolina prison.

And, we are not the only country to feel this threat. A July, 2013, NATO Industrial Advisory Group, Study Group 170, "Engagement of Low, Slow and Small Aerial Targets by Ground Based Air Defense," concludes that, "If appropriate measures are taken in the near future it will be possible to significantly mitigate the threat that LSS [low, slow, small] platforms pose to any future military conflict or from the terrorist attack of national infrastructure." Other NATO study groups have jumped into this issue, but participation by U.S. companies and the Government in these on-going studies appears underrepresented.

The United Kingdom took this threat so seriously in 2012 that the Royal Air Force, and Selex ES, designed and deployed an integrated counter sUAS system in London to defend the Olympic Stadium, particularly during the opening ceremonies. This system was further improved and used to defend world leaders during the 2013 G8 Summit in Enniskillen, Scotland, and, most recently, at the 2014 NATO Summit in Wales. Certainly, the lessons learned from these efforts should inform our actions as we address this common threat.

ROADMAP TOWARDS A U.S. SOLUTION

Technology typically outstrips policies, and this technology has certainly stretched the capacity of the U.S. Government's bureaucracy to swiftly provide a counter drone strategy. Thus, we find ourselves behind in strategy, policy, and the technological capabilities needed to counter-sUAS's. Hence, this two-pronged problem requires a simultaneous, two-track solution.

First, a search should be conducted to find technology that has already been developed, tested, refined, and used operationally. By using a combination of radar, networked electronic support measures, infrared, electro optical cameras, and engagement solutions of electronic attack, or hard kill options, the threat can be neutralized and the physical and electronic forensic evidence can be preserved for arrest and prosecution.

This system should consist of an integrated network of multiple layered means of defense to find, fix, track, identify and classify, then engage and assess the result. It should also be designed for persistent, low-profile surveillance and be operational 24/7/365. This system should also incorporate a rapid decision-making process that can be used to quickly prosecute a response since one of the unique abilities of sUAS's is to quickly close on a target with little notice. The system must also possess a range of "soft" and kinetic responses, both with a high "Probability of Kill." The counter system that is selected must also be able to capture and preserve the appropriate incident information that will inevitably be used for prosecuting the sUAS operators.

Additionally, the system must be able to fully operate without interfering with security, law enforcement, or first responder networks and communications. Thus, the system must be able to comply with Federal Communication Commission rules, if not operating under special rules for highly sensitive areas. The system should also have a variant that is mobile (man-portable and air-transportable) for temporary setups. Of course, the system must be designed with open architecture in order to allow for spiral, scalable, and modular developments as drone technology continues to evolve (i.e., 5G LTE will almost immediately offer new capabilities to command and control drones). Finally, any system must be economically proportionate to the threat and available almost immediately.

The second step of this two-pronged solution starts with interagency cooperation to draft an overarching strategy and linked policies that have a legal and regulatory basis to deal with drones. A single department or agency should be charged with leading this effort using the experiences and lessons learned from our international allies as they have already wrestled with these issues. In any case, it will take a joined effort across all Government departments since it will require navigating through current rules and regulations in the face of the unique capabilities of sUAS's and recommending changes to those base documents. For example, even though drones are unmanned, they are currently considered "aircraft" by the FAA and are protected by all of the laws and rules associated with manned flight when they are airborne. This is just one example of where current policy could severely limit options in reacting to a drone attack.

Once formalized, the overarching goals of the strategy and individual policies would then lead to identifying the correct supporting tactics, techniques, and procedures needed to guide security and law enforcement personnel during their response to any threat. The goal, of course, is to mitigate the safety and security risks while steering this technology towards its positive and productive uses.

RECOMMENDATIONS

1. Draft a single strategy and supporting policies that clearly guide Government agencies in regards to Rules of Engagement and ensure that all responses are proportionate to the threat.

2. Simultaneously work with allies and international partners to discover "lessons learned" and best practices for solutions to the counter-drone issue.

3. Rapidly acquire proven technical solutions that can immediately provide protection to National critical infrastructure and personnel.

4. Train and educate Federal law enforcement, and State and local law enforcement, personnel on the legal uses of drones, and potential threats.

5. Conduct a campaign to educate the public (sUAS operators and non-operators) on the use, and potential misuse, of drones.

6. Work closely with commercial drone manufacturers to install geo-fencing and traceability codes into drones of specific capabilities (i.e., size, weight, battery/motor size, flight times, etc.)

7. Draft appropriate legislation and regulations that govern the registration, licensing, etc. of any manufactured, or home-built, drone that fall above a specified weight and/or capabilities.

8. Establish, and fund, an on-going research and development program to devise counters to new drone technologies before they widely appear in the marketplace.

With last week's announcement by the Secret Service that the White House grounds would be used to conduct a series of exercises involving drones, it is clear the United States is not fully ready to deal with the threats that could come from this emerging technology today. However, there is a path to success. By capitalizing on "best practices" already discovered by our international allies, such as the United Kingdom, we could be ready to deal with today's threats immediately, while we draft the correct policies and spin up U.S. industries and laboratories to rapidly explore ways to counter tomorrow's drones and their unique, new, threats.

Mr. PERRY. Thank you, Mr. Roggero.

The Chairman now recognizes Chief Beary for your testimony, sir.

STATEMENT OF RICHARD BEARY, PRESIDENT, INTERNATIONAL ASSOCIATION OF CHIEFS OF POLICE

Chief BEARY. Good morning, Chairman Perry and Members of the subcommittee. Thank you for inviting me to testify today on the potential threat posed by unmanned aerial systems.

As president of the International Association of Chiefs of Police, commonly referred to as the IACP, and on behalf of our 23,000 members in 98 different countries, I would like to thank you, Members of this committee, for the support you have demonstrated for law enforcement over the years. Our law enforcement community and our communities in general need your support. Thank you.

The IACP is the world's largest association of law enforcement leaders, and for over 120 years the IACP has been launching internationally-acclaimed programs, speaking out on behalf of law enforcement, and conducting ground-breaking research. We provide services not only in the United States but across the globe.

I began my law enforcement career in 1977 and, as the Chairman said, I have 30 years on the municipal side, and now I have almost 8 years on the university side of law enforcement. The University of Central Florida is the largest university in the State of Florida, and we are the second-largest in the United States.

During my career I have watched the threats to our communities evolve. We still deal with the problem of violent crime, drugs, prostitution, smuggling, trafficking, and gangs, but we are now tasked in dealing with cyber threats, violent extremism, terrorism, and highly organized criminals with access to specialized equipment to aid them in their mission and to harm others and devastate our communities.

Included in that specialized equipment are unmanned aerial systems. While UAS can be a great tool, they also pose a serious threat to the public and law enforcement when used by the wrong people.

When used responsibly, and with good policies in place, UAS have enhanced law enforcement's ability to protect communities they serve. UAS has helped law enforcement agencies save time, save money, and, most importantly, save lives.

They are ideal for dangerous or difficult situations, like executing high-risk warrants; responding to barricaded suspects; gaining situational awareness in difficult terrain; and enhancing officer safety by exposing unseen dangers; locating missing children; or responding to damage caused by emergencies such as natural disasters, downed power lines, or hazardous material incidents.

Despite the undeniable benefits these systems can have, they also pose a grave threat to public safety. Almost anyone can obtain an unmanned aerial system these days. They can buy it off the shelf from Amazon, have it delivered in 2 days, charge the battery, and immediately begin flying the device.

The fact that these devices are so readily available to the public is concerning. The average citizen that is purchasing these devices generally has no aviation experience and therefore does not think twice about operating in controlled airspace, over the public, or over a crowded beach or any other gathering—mass gathering. Nor do they think twice about launching a UAS to ascertain what the police or the fire department is working on up the street.

This is a real danger to the public. Public safety and others regarding these aircraft have to be addressed. The average citizen simply does not know what they are doing wrong and the potential damaging effects that these devices can have when operated improperly.

Recently we have witnessed several high-profile incidents with UAS. Of course, we talked about the crash landing at the White House, flying over sensitive locations, and near-miss with aircraft on a regular basis. At the University of Central Florida we have personally experienced these aircraft flying over mass gatherings, including football games, in violation of airspace restrictions that are in place to protect the public.

The newest version of these devices are now flown in virtual reality mode, meaning that the operator does not need to be in the line of sight while flying the aircraft.

Thankfully, at this point most of the incidents involving UAS have not lead to horrific events, but I don't think we are far away from one of those happening. The concerns are real. There is nothing to stop the criminal element from purchasing a UAS and using it to cause localized or catastrophic damage.

I mentioned earlier that I am from Orlando, which is home to many, many theme parks. I can assure you they have major concerns about the safety of their guests, and they have numerous incidents of these devices flying over their airspace. They have a real fear that someone wants to harm a large amount of people who are attending their parks.

Now, something as simple as a UAS were to fly into a park or a football stadium with something as simple as a smoke bomb could cause incredible panic, thus leading to major injuries for the people that are there.

Again, these devices can be used to fly over restricted areas and to plan an attack.

Because these devices are in their infancy, now is the time for the Federal Government and the Federal agencies to work with us and develop the guidelines so that law enforcement knows what to do. The Department of Homeland Security did provide my agency with a 2-page document on recommended UAS response procedures at our stadium. We got that late in the football season in November.

While those things are nice, there is no detail in what do we do for the follow-up, how do we respond to these, who do we call for further information? We are not criticizing the Federal Government; this is our call for help. Law enforcement needs to know how you want us to respond to these and where we are going to go in the future.

The lack of clear guidance and best practices has led to confusion among the law enforcement community when they are dealing with these. Almost every critical situation now, they are drones flying over top of law enforcement officers and interfering with our helicopter when we are trying to deal with these things.

Again, since these devices do not have a transponder or a registration, it is difficult to track down and it is impossible, in many cases, to figure out where they came from.

Without law enforcement knowing the proper procedures it leaves us vulnerable and makes our primary job of keeping the public safe more challenging.

Ladies and gentlemen, I thank you for allowing me the opportunity to be here. I look forward to the questions.

Again, I bring quite a bit of law enforcement experience to the table, and if you want to talk about the Justice report, wherever you want to go I am good to go. Thank you.

[The prepared statement of Chief Beary follows:]

PREPARED STATEMENT OF RICHARD BEARY

MARCH 18, 2015

Good morning Chairman Perry and Members of the subcommittee: Thank you for inviting me to testify today on the potential threat posed by unmanned aerial systems. As president of the International Association of Chiefs of Police (IACP), and on behalf of our over 23,000 members in 98 different countries, I would like to thank this committee and subcommittee for the support it has demonstrated over the years for the law enforcement field and our communities.

The IACP is the world's largest association of law enforcement leaders. For over 120 years, the IACP has been launching internationally-acclaimed programs, speaking out on behalf of law enforcement, conducting ground-breaking research, and providing exemplary programs and services to the law enforcement profession around the globe.

I began my law enforcement career in 1977, and I am now chief of police for the University of Central Florida, the largest university in the State and the second in the country. During my career, I have watched the threats to our communities evolve. We still dealing with the problem of violent crime, drugs, prostitution, smuggling/trafficking, and gangs. We are now dealing with cyber threats, violent extremism, terrorism, and highly-organized criminals with access to specialized equipment to aid them in their mission to harm others and devastate our communities.

Included in that specialized equipment are Unmanned Aerial Systems (UAS). While UAS can be a great tool they also pose a serious threat to the public and law enforcement when used by the wrong people. When used responsibly, and with good policies in place, UAS have enhanced law enforcement's ability to protect the communities they serve. UAS have helped law enforcement agencies save time, save money, and most importantly, save lives. They are ideal for dangerous or difficult situations like executing high-risk warrants; responding to barricaded subjects; gaining situational awareness in difficult terrain; enhancing officer safety by exposing unseen dangers; locating a missing child; or responding to the damage caused by emergencies such as natural disasters, downed power lines, or hazardous material incidents.

Despite the undeniable benefits UAS can have, they can also pose a grave threat to public safety. Almost anyone can get ahold of an unmanned aerial system these days. You can buy an off-the-shelf product from Amazon, have it delivered in 2 days, charge the battery, and immediately begin flying the device. The fact that these devices are so readily available to the public is concerning. The average citizen that is purchasing these devices generally has no aviation experience, and therefore does not think twice about operating them in controlled airspaces, over the public or on a crowded beach. Nor do they think twice about launching a UAS to ascertain what the police or fire department is working on up the street. This is the real danger to the public, public safety, and others regarding these aircraft. The average citizen simply does not know what they are doing wrong and the potential damaging effects these devices can have if not operated properly.

Recently we have witnessed several high-profile incidents with UAS—crash landing on the White House lawn, flying over sensitive Federal buildings or locations, or having near-miss incidents with an aircraft. At the University of Central Florida, we have experienced these aircrafts flying over mass gatherings, including football games, in violation of airspace restrictions. The newest version of these devices are flown in virtual reality mode, meaning the operator does not need to be in the line of sight while flying the craft.

23

Thankfully, at this point, most of the incidents involving UAS have not lead to horrific events, but I don't think we are far away from seeing more incidents involving unmanned aerial systems that lead to tragedy. The concerns out there are real. There is nothing to stop the criminal element from purchasing a UAS and using it to cause localized or catastrophic damage. I mentioned earlier that a local theme park has witnessed UAS flying over the park. They have the real fear that someone who wants to harm a large amount of people could use a UAS to do this. If a UAS were to drop something as simple as a smoke bomb down on a theme park or during a football game, think of the panic that could ensue. These devices can also be used to fly over sensitive areas and gather information for a planned attack; to disperse a chemical/radiological agent; and to conduct an explosive attack.

Because the use and availability of UAS in its infancy, the guidance around how law enforcement agencies should respond to and mitigate potential UAS threats is relatively nonexistent. The Federal Aviation Administration (FAA) has issued guidance to the law enforcement community explaining the legal framework for the agency's oversight of aviation safety in the United States, including UAS operations, how UAS can be operated legally, and the options for legal enforcement actions against unauthorized or unsafe UAS operators. The Department of Homeland Security did provide my agency with a 2-page document on recommended UAS response procedures at our stadium. The DHS guide includes recommended response to a UAS in a stadium and outside a stadium, potential illicit uses of a UAS, recommended pre-event measures, and a brief overview of the FAA guidelines. Other than those two documents, law enforcement has had little guidance on response procedures. This is not a criticism to our Federal agency partners, it is a call for help.

The lack of clear guidance and best practices has led to confusion among the law enforcement community regarding about what law enforcement is allowed to do when they encounter a UAS. Tactical guidance needs to be provided on the proper measures to take.

Since these devices do not have a transponder device, registration number, or other mechanism to track them, it makes them next to impossible to identify when they are flown or who is flying them. What steps can we take to identify UAS and the operators of these devices? If we see a device being flown somewhere it should not be, can we bring it down? These questions only scratch the surface, and many of my fellow law enforcement officers are asking themselves these tough questions.

Without law enforcement knowing the proper procedures that need to occur, it leaves us vulnerable and makes our primary job of keeping the public safe from harm more challenging.

Mr. PERRY. Thank you, Chief Beary.

The Chairman now recognizes Dr. McNeal for your testimony, sir.

STATEMENT OF GREGORY S. MCNEAL, ASSOCIATE PROFESSOR, SCHOOL OF LAW, PEPPERDINE UNIVERSITY

Mr. MCNEAL. Chairman Perry, Ranking Member Watson Coleman, Ranking Member Thompson, and Members of the committee, thank you for hosting this hearing and inviting me to testify.

The emergence of unmanned aerial vehicles in domestic skies raises understandable concerns that may require employment of mitigation technologies by law enforcement or security personnel. However, before any funds are expended on such technologies, agencies should engage in comprehensive risk assessment to identify the probability of that harm, the magnitude of a potential harm, benefits of security measures, and the cost of those measures. We have to bear in mind that one of the significant costs is that the vast majority of drones will be used for economically and socially beneficial purposes, and we have to remain cognizant of that at all points in time.

This testimony outlines four key issues that Congress should remain cognizant of when drafting legislation or overseeing the Department of Homeland Security.

First, Congress should ensure that agencies are distinguishing between possible threats, which we can all sit around and imagine, and probable threats. Congress should also ensure that agencies are avoiding fear-based appeals that might drive the policymaking process.

Drones are an exciting topic. They capture the attention of the media. Oftentimes that drives agencies to feel like they need to do something, to look like they are responding.

The recent attention for drones, though, oftentimes appears to be driven by this type of media attention. I say this because while remote control aircraft are seemingly new, they have, in fact, been around for decades.

Furthermore, the small quadcopters that have been gathering so much attention lately due to their ease of use would also be the least useful to a dedicated attacker. Rather, larger, faster, and heavier systems exist, and these systems have existed for many years. Many of those systems can be home-built, and in the hands of a dedicated attacker they will be very difficult to stop.

Given the complexity of the threat picture, we must ensure that agencies do not fall victim to the sensationalism that drives worst-case scenario-based planning. Such an approach to risk management can justify enormous expenditures no matter how unlikely the prospects are that the event will take place.

We should avoid focusing only on the extreme but improbable, and rather, we should do the best that we can to focus on the probable and assess the magnitude of the potential harm that might flow from those.

Second, Congress should ensure that agencies are assessing risk by not only looking at that probability of a successful attack, but also the magnitude of losses. Congress should ensure that every agency action related to an alleged homeland security risk from drones is preceded by a risk assessment. That is the first step in any managerial decision about potential threats. Across homeland security, any time we are looking at threats it should be preceded by looking at the risk before we immediately begin expending funds.

A risk assessment is that first step and ensures that agencies make hard choices with limited resources. Every possible threat cannot be guarded against; therefore, agencies have to focus on the riskiest threats.

Third, Congress should ensure that before any funds are spent agencies are also engaged in a formal cost-benefit analysis. The employment of mitigation technology against risk cannot take place in a vacuum. Rather, it requires agencies to consider the degree to which a security measure is likely to deter, disrupt, or protect against a terrorist attack.

The reality is that implementing security measures across all— across the Federal Government will require aggregating the costs across thousands of facilities. How to allocate those scarce resources will require prioritization driven by risk assessments, and this brings me to my final point.

Congress should ensure that specific individuals at the Department of Homeland Security are responsible for conducting these analyses and reporting their methodology. Congress may also want to provide funds to the Centers of Excellence for an independent check on how agencies are conducting these assessments.

Given the complexity of the risk assessment picture associated with drones and their potential to pose a homeland security threat, I am certain that DHS and agencies are working on this. I am sure many people are working on this. In fact, that might be part of the problem is that in every—in each stovepipe across agencies, various individuals might be working on the threat but there is not a single point of coordination.

So Congress should direct that a specific individual or an office within DHS take the interagency lead on this. There is some precedent for this. Back in 2004 homeland security stood up an office known as the Counter-MANPADS System Program Office. This was the office that assessed whether or not there was a threat to commercial aviation from man-portable surface-to-air missiles.

It was a temporary office that assessed the threat; after assessing the threat, providing some recommendations, it went away.

We could stand up a similar office about emerging threats. Or in the alternative, what we could do is we could designate that the under secretary for National Protection and Programs Directorate lead a threat assessment process for drones specifically, or for emerging threats in general.

The emergence of unmanned aerial vehicles in domestic skies raises understandable concerns, but before any funds are expended on such technologies—mitigation technologies, the Department should engage in a comprehensive risk assessment to identify the probability of harm, magnitude of harm, benefits of security measures, and the direct and indirect costs of those security measures.

Thank you.

[The prepared statement of Dr. McNeal follows:]

PREPARED STATEMENT OF GREGORY S. MCNEAL

MARCH 18, 2015

INTRODUCTION

The emergence of unmanned aerial vehicles in domestic skies raises understandable concerns that may require employment of mitigation technologies. However, before any funds are expended on such technologies, the Department of Homeland Security should engage in a comprehensive risk assessment to identify the probability, magnitude of harm, benefits of security measures, and cost of those measures. This testimony outlines four key issues that Congress should remain cognizant of when drafting legislation and/or overseeing the activities of the Department of Homeland Security.

RECOMMENDATIONS

(1) Congress should ensure that agencies are distinguishing between possible threats and probable threats; Congress should also ensure that agencies are avoiding fear-based appeals focused on worst-case scenarios: Drones are an exciting topic that captures the interest of journalists and the public. The popular attention associated with drones has the benefit of raising awareness about their potential uses, however it also raises the possibility that emotions and sensationalism will drive the crafting of public policy.

For example, after a recreational drone crashed on the White House lawn, ''security experts'' appeared on CNN to discuss the possibility that a drone might be equipped with explosives or weapons of mass destruction. This is a highly unlikely scenario. While consumer drones are readily available, lightweight explosives and weapons of mass destruction are not. Even if terrorists were able to procure explosives or WMD, using a consumer drone to conduct an attack would be one of the least effective means of carrying out an attack. Nevertheless, the Secret Service and other agencies seem to be planning for ''possible'' worst-case scenarios. Such an approach shifts the policy debate away from probability and creates demands for substantial Governmental responses even when the risk does not warrant the response.[1]

Congress must ensure that agencies do not fall victim to the sensationalism that drives worst-case scenario-based planning. Such an approach to risk management can justify enormous expenditures, no matter how unlikely the prospects are that the dire event will take place. As security analyst Bruce Schneier has written, focusing on the worst possible outcome ''substitutes imagination for thinking, speculation for risk analysis, and fear for reason.''[2] It substitutes ill-informed possibilistic thinking over careful, well-reasoned, probabilistic thinking, forcing us to focus on what we don't know, and what we can imagine, rather than what we do know. ''By speculating about what can possibly go wrong, and then acting as if that is likely to happen, worst-case thinking focuses only on the extreme but improbable risks and does a poor job at assessing outcomes.''[3]

Congress should ensure that agencies are as concerned with the probability of harm as they are of the possibility of a worst-case scenario. This requires paying attention to the ''spectrum of threats, not simply the worst one imaginable, in order to properly understand and coherently deal with the risks to people, institutions, and the economy.'' While public attention to the issue of drones may create a sense of urgency amongst members of the public and some agency officials, this ''does not relieve those in charge of the requirement, even the duty, to make decisions about the expenditures of vast quantities of public monies in a responsible manner'' that is disconnected from emotions and focused on probabilities.[4]

(2) Congress should ensure that agencies are assessing risk by calculating both the probability of a successful attack and the magnitude of losses that might be sustained in a successful attack: Congress should ensure that every agency action related to an alleged homeland security risk from drones is preceded by a risk assessment. Assessing risks is the first managerial step in decision making about potential threats, and it is one that is readily subject to Congressional oversight. Forcing agencies to conduct a risk assessment is the first step toward ensuring that agencies efficiently and effectively use taxpayer funds and control costs. A risk assessment is also the first step toward ensuring that agencies make hard choices with limited resources—every possible threat cannot be guarded against, therefore agencies must focus on the riskiest threats.

''Risk is the expected consequences of a terrorist attack, and the accepted definition of risk as applied in the terrorism context, is *Risk* = *(probability of a successful attack)* × *(losses sustained in the successful attack).*''[5] *Probability of successful attack* in this context is the likelihood of a successful terrorist attack using a drone if the security measure were not in place. On the probability side of the equation, the benefits of drones are that they allow an adversary to control delivery of an attack from a distance, perhaps solving some operational problems (like risk of capture) that terrorists may face in planning and mounting an operation. However, they introduce complexity into the attackers operation that may decrease the likelihood of a successful attack. The clear advantages of drones are that they allow for: (1) Attacks over perimeter defenses, (2) multiple simultaneous attacks without directly risking attacker personnel, (3) better surveillance capabilities. However, the probability of a successful attack may also go down when an attacker chooses to use a drone. In fact, one RAND/Defense Threat Reduction Agency study found:

''[UAVs] do not appear to have major advantages over other ways of carrying out operations against similar targets, although they cannot be dismissed outright as a potential threat. Where they did appear preferable, the choice for these systems was driven by the actions of the defense or in place security measures—i.e., were alternative attack modes foreclosed by defenses or did concerns about a potentially compromised plan push the attacking group farther away from its desired targets? The price of these advantages was, however, greater complexity, technological uncertainty, and higher cost and risks associated with these platforms. Consequently, rather than being an attack mode likely to be widely embraced by such actors,

---

[1] Sunstein, Cass R. 2003. Terrorism and Probability Neglect. *Journal of Risk and Uncertainty* (26)(2–3) March–May: 121–136.
[2] Schneier, Bruce. 2003. *Beyond Fear: Thinking Sensibly about Security in an Uncertain World.* New York: Copernicus.
[3] *Id.*
[4] Mueller, John and Stewart, Mark G. 2011. *Terror, Security, and Money.* New York: Oxford University Press.
[5] *Id.*

UAVs . . . appear to represent a 'niche threat'—potentially making some contribution to the overall asymmetric and terrorist threat . . . UAVs do provide some advantages to an attacker, but in most cases there are simpler alternatives that provide similar, or even superior, capabilities.''[6]

Losses sustained in the successful attack in this context include the fatalities and other damage (both direct and indirect) that will accrue as a result of a successful terrorist attack employing a drone.[7] This part of the calculation takes account of the value and vulnerability of people and infrastructure, as well as any psychological and political effects. Thus, agencies engaging in an analysis of risk must separate the probability that an attack will be successful if committed using a drone (the subject of the preceding paragraph) from the magnitude of harm that would flow from that particular attack if it were successful.

Thus the prior factor, *probability of successful attack*, would address the low likelihood that an attacker would be able to acquire explosives or WMD, and the decreased likelihood of success with explosives or WMD when using a drone versus alternative methods (like delivering from a manned aircraft, a vehicle, or carried by a person). Whereas the losses sustained factor assumes the scenario analyzed probabilistically is successful, and looks to what harms would then flow. In the context of drones, this will requiring gathering information about the payload capabilities of various systems (if assessing a threat from explosives), or the dispersal capability of various systems (if assessing a threat from WMD). What analysts will likely find is that the low payload capabilities of drones will reduce the direct losses sustained from an attack, however the propaganda value associated with a drone attack may increase the indirect costs (such as psychological, economic, and political effects) associated with their use.

Taken together, the probability of a successful attack employing a drone multiplied by the losses sustained in the successful attack will tell agencies what the risk from drones is. From there agencies, guided by Congress, can determine whether the risk is acceptable. If the risk is unacceptable, then agencies should adopt mitigation, risk reduction, and security measures to reduce the risk to an acceptable level— remaining cognizant of the fact that such measures have costs (the subject of the next section).

(3) Congress should ensure that before any funds are spent on security measures, agencies engage in risk assessment and a formal cost-benefit analysis using best practices: The employment of mitigation technology against risks cannot take place in a vacuum. Rather, it requires agencies to consider the degree to which a security measure is likely to deter, disrupt, or protect against a terrorist attack. Mitigation technologies are thus a benefit that can reduce risk (as calculated in the prior section).[8] To determine the benefit of a security measure, agencies should make the following calculation: *Benefit of a security measure = (probability of a successful attack) × (losses sustained in the successful attack) × (reduction in risk generated by the security measure).*[9]

The first two factors in this equation are identical to those calculated earlier, while the *reduction in risk* factor is a degree, or percentage factor. In the context of drones, reductions in risk may come from greater surveillance of areas near airports where drones might pose a risk to commercial aircraft, or it may be specific technologies designed to jam the communication links between drones and their operators. But all of the likely risk reduction security measures will have costs, and sometimes those costs may be significant. Thus, the costs will need to be compared to the *benefit of a security measure*. A hypothetical will help illustrate this analytical process.

Hypothetical

FACTS: Assume that in a 10-year span of time we believe there is a chance of one successful attack by an explosives-laden drone against a Federal facility (a 10% yearly chance). Suppose further that we believe an attack will result in 1 death (valued at $10 million, an admittedly high estimate), and significant psychological and economic damage (valued at $50 million, an admittedly high estimate). For this hypothetical the total losses from such an attack amount to $60 million.

RISK: The yearly *risk* from such an attack is thus the (*probability of a successful attack* .10) × (*losses sustained in a successful attack* $60 million)=$6 million.

---

[6] Jackson, Brian A. et.al. 2008. *Evaluating Novel Threats To The Homeland*, RAND.
[7] Mueller, John and Stewart, Mark G. 2011. *Terror, Security, and Money*. New York: Oxford University Press.
[8] *Id.*
[9] *Id.*

BENEFIT OF SECURITY: Now assume that a security system can be installed that cuts the probability of a successful attack by 50%. Such a system might be a combination of cameras, sensors, and jamming equipment that allows for detection of a drone and the jamming of the drone's control link.

The yearly *benefit of the security measure* is the reduction in risk associated with its employment, which is thus the (*probability of a successful attack* .10) × (*losses sustained in a successful attack* $60 million) × (*reduction in risk generated by the security measure* .50)=$3 million.

IS THE COST OF SECURITY WORTH IT?: To determine whether the cost of such a security system is worth the expenditure of taxpayer dollars, we must compare the costs to the benefits. If the cost of cameras, sensors, and an interdiction system for drones in this hypothetical were less than $3 million, the benefits would outweigh the costs, and it would be a cost-effective security measure.

Importantly, this hypothetical calculation only takes account of the security measures being implemented at one Federal facility. The reality is that implementing such measures across the Federal Government will require aggregating the costs across thousands of facilities. How to allocate those scarce resources will require prioritization, driven by risk assessments (as explained above), and will require the identification of a specific individual or office within the Department of Homeland Security responsible for coordinating interagency efforts to conduct risk assessments.

(4) Congress should ensure that specific individuals at the Department of Homeland Security are responsible for conducting these analyses and reporting their methodology. Congress may also want to provide funds to the Centers of Excellence for an independent evaluation of threats: Given the complexity of the risk assessment picture associated with drones and their potential to pose a homeland security threat, Congress should direct that a specific individual or office within the Department of Homeland Security assume responsibility for generating threat assessments.

There is some precedent for this type of managerial approach. In 2004, the Department of Homeland Security initiated a $100 million program to evaluate whether civilian aircraft should be equipped with countermeasures to defeat the threat of man-portable surface-to-air missiles. The program was directed by Congress as a means to evaluate whether Congress should require that some or all U.S. commercial airliners install such devices. At the time, the office within DHS was known as the Counter-MANPADS System Program Office. Congress could create a similar temporary office within DHS for the purpose of evaluating the threat posed by unmanned aircraft. In the alternative, Congress could direct the under secretary, National Protection & Programs Directorate to lead and staff a similar effort within DHS and make the under secretary the lead Federal official for interagency efforts.

Additionally, Congress may want to consider requesting the support of the Department of Homeland Security Centers of Excellence. These university-based research centers can engage in terrorism risk analyses that will supplement the work of DHS. Such outside research may provide an independent check on the interests of Government agencies that may adopt or promote drone countermeasures as a means to ensure the continued relevance of their office or to justify increased budgetary outlays.[10]

CONCLUSION

The emergence of unmanned aerial vehicles in domestic skies raises understandable concerns that may require employment of mitigation technologies. However, before any funds are expended on such technologies, the Department of Homeland Security should engage in a comprehensive risk assessment to identify the probability, magnitude of harm, benefits of security measures, and cost of those measures.

Mr. PERRY. Thank you, Dr. McNeal.

The Chairman now recognizes himself for a few questions. I will start out with General Roggero.

According to a January 2015 *Wall Street Journal* article, counter-terrorism authorities in the United States, Germany, Spain, and Egypt stated that six potential terrorist plots involving drones had been foiled since 2011. Can you describe, if you know, the types of

---

[10] For an example of such mismanagement, see GAO Report, *DOD Needs Strategic Outcome-Related Goals and Visibility over Its Counter-IED Efforts* available at: *http://www.gao.gov/assets/590/588804.pdf*.

29

capabilities of the UAS that these groups were using or planning to use?

General ROGERRO. Sir, I am sorry about that.

Mr. PERRY. Sure.

General ROGERRO. No, sir, I am not familiar with the technology that they used in that particular case.

Mr. PERRY. Okay.

Anybody else on the panel, just in case?

Yes, sir, Dr. Humphreys.

Mr. HUMPHREYS. I do know that commercial off-the-shelf technology, when modified, is perfectly capable of carrying out those kind of attacks. In fact, even as we speak, in Ukraine the conflict is involving off-the-shelf drone hardware modified for that conflict, for surveillance and even weaponized drones.

So it is probably the case that they were using an open-source autopilot and off-the-shelf hardware.

Mr. PERRY. So surveillance is pretty simple. You mount a camera, or you can buy one with a camera mounted.

Dr. Humphreys or General Roggero, can you talk to us about the weaponization or other potential nefarious means—to be combative or proactive in a militaristic style?

Mr. HUMPHREYS. Right now surveillance is being used in Ukraine to guide mortar shelling.

Mr. PERRY. Okay.

Mr. HUMPHREYS. So it can be, you know, part of the lethal chain.

Mr. PERRY. Sure.

Mr. HUMPHREYS. But beyond that you can, of course, insert in the battery compartment some explosives. Many of these drones can carry a couple of pounds easily.

Of course, if your intention is to cause panic, as was mentioned earlier, all you have to do is drop a smoke bomb and you can cause that kind of panic.

General ROGERRO. So there are other things that you can do with that, as well. Mobility is one.

For example, in Congressman Loudermilk's State, delivering marijuana and cell phones into prisons has been attempted. I believe just a few weeks back there was 6½ pounds of crystal meth being delivered across the border from the Tijuana area into San Ysidro. So certainly smuggling is an activity that is being seen out there with these particular devices.

But certainly intelligence-gathering, surveillance, and reconnaissance is the top priority and the easily done thing with these drones. We have also seen ISIS use it very effectively to do propaganda and broadcast after an attack, as well, to use these devices to gain their images that they need to put out on the web.

Mr. PERRY. Okay. Thank you.

To Professor McNeal: As we have discussed today, the UAS can be used for a variety of malicious purposes and therefore present a multitude of potential threats. The DHS will often prepare risk assessments in the face of threats such as these to ensure all relevant stakeholders are taking all possible steps to mitigate the threat.

Which areas do you perceive the threats are most pressing and why, if you know?

Mr. McNeal. It is difficult to answer that question without a direct view of the intelligence picture, but let me answer it in a general way and—which sort of focuses on the capabilities of UAVs and how I think the threat assessment process should approach it.

Really, UAVs provide three distinct advantages. They allow for attacks over perimeter defenses, and so when you think of the hardening that we did for Federal facilities after 9/11 and after the Oklahoma City bombings, now the enemy is able to attack beyond—over those perimeter defenses. If you have an area that is intended to be secure, either from observation or from personnel trafficking through, because you have fences, UAV obviously can get over that.

Second, better surveillance capabilities, which we have already discussed. It gives a different vantage point.

Then third, also allows the possibility of multiple simultaneous attacks or multiple disruptive attacks. So if you have a gathering—a crowded gathering, as Chief Beary mentioned, you might—if I were an attacker I might send in multiple drones with smoke bombs to create—to get people moved from a secure perimeter to outside of a secure perimeter where I might engage in an attack.

All these things, of course, are possibilities that you could do as an individual on the ground. In fact, the limitation of UAVs is the payload. So the typical UAV might be able to carry 5 pounds of explosives. You could have one that carries more than that, but you are really starting to get into more sophisticated systems.

Whereas a person can carry 20 pounds of explosives if they are—if they bring it in on a backpack. They don't have to be a suicide bomber; they could leave it in a facility. Of course, we can mitigate that with security checks.

So the security threat picture needs to balance not only the capabilities that the enemy gets by using this in an attack factor, but then also some of the limitations on it. That is why I say that we need a comprehensive process to assess each threat across each facility in each type of scenario.

Mr. Perry. Thank you. My time is expired.

The Chairman now recognizes the Ranking Member, Mrs. Watson Coleman, for questions.

Mrs. Watson Coleman. Thank you very much, Mr. Chairman.

Thank you very much for your testimony. One thing that you all have raised in my mind is that there is this sort of drone capacity from the tiniest to the biggest. So I need to know what I should be worried about.

The drone that could possibly create a threat, whether or not it is, you know, disseminating some gas or some weaponization or whatever, what is the smallest drone, and what is the average cost of that type of drone? Because I am trying to figure out what don't we bother ourselves with.

I don't even know who can answer that, but if anyone of you want to take a shot at it——

Mr. Humphreys. I will jump in first. I bought a drone for my son for Christmas that was no bigger than my hand. I don't think we have to worry about that one.

But we do have to keep in mind that the threshold for success in these attacks can be very low. If anything exploded due to a drone acting on the White House, even though it didn't cause much physical damage, that would be viewed as a successful attack. You know, it would cause psychological and economic damage.

So in that case, they don't have to be much bigger than the one that I bought for my son for Christmas, and——

Mrs. WATSON COLEMAN. So then I guess my question is: How do we go about discerning what we should be concerned about, and how we should be—policy should be evolving and interagency inter-action, you know, taking place so that we are prioritizing our response and our proactivity in this area, at the same time recognizing it has—these have very important economic benefits. They help farmers with their crops, they—certainly an industry that has the potential to be very, very successful, and we can certainly use that economy here.

What is it that we should be doing? Are we now facing impediments because FAA has got a piece of this, DHS has a piece of this, Secret Service has a piece of this? You know, is anybody cooperating?

Mr. MCNEAL. Congresswoman Coleman, I think this highlights the challenge that we all face, which is the spectrum of risk is from the smallest UAV up to extremely large 55-pound systems that could fly at 200 miles an hour and they are systems filled with fuel. But these have existed for decades.

So for us to recognize the possible is, I think, really that first moment at which then we turn to homeland security and we say, "It is time for you to have a comprehensive process where you study this." We do this all the time across Government, right? We pass a new bill that directs an agency to engage in scientific studies to figure out whether the benefits of adding a certain device to an automobile are worth it.

That same type of scientific process has to be applied here.

Mrs. WATSON COLEMAN. Should that be sort-of our starting point?

Mr. MCNEAL. I think that should be our starting point. I think we have recognized the potential and that a lot more research is required for us to do something.

The best thing for us to do is to begin that process inside Government of making those studies and making informed decisions. Otherwise what I think and I fear will happen is that the next drone that crashes on the White House lawn has a firecracker on it and we say, "What if it were something worse?" and we make hasty decisions that aren't informed by science.

Mrs. WATSON COLEMAN. So, Mr. Roggero—I hope I didn't bastardize your name—you shared information with regard to our international partners around the world, and they are—they seem to be a little bit farther along than we are. So what are the lessons that we specifically need to learn from them as we embark on this year?

General ROGERRO. Thank you very much for that. One of the things that they learned—they started back in 2012—their trigger event, if you will, was the 2012 Olympics, and that is what they were concerned about—was that there is no single silver bullet that is going to apply. As you yourself said, it is a spectrum of threat, and one of the first things you have to do is catalogue that threat and identify it, and then go through the mitigation strategies that can be put against it.

But one of the most important things that they discovered was that the defense had to be layered. It had to be a combination of things, as Dr. Humphreys was mentioning. It is not just electro-optical cameras and radars and thermal, but a whole slew—menu of things that you need to protect those vitally important parts and gatherings that we do have.

Mrs. WATSON COLEMAN. Thank you, Mr. Chairman. I have one more question, if I might? Thank you very much.

This is, Chief Beary, you did—you illustrated the good and the bad of drones in law enforcement, and I was just wondering, with regard to what we learned in the Ferguson matter, is there any use for them in ensuring accountability, fairness, and protection of communities other than, you know, using them as revenue sources?

Chief BEARY. Well, on the revenue source side, I am not sure that there is any of those that exist now. I can tell you this, being a person who spent 30 years in municipal government, quite frankly, the operations out there were—trying to use taxpayers to fund your system is wrong.

I will tell you this as a police chief: Every police chief in this country works for a mayor and a city commission, or whatever the word is in your community, and they need to be held accountable, plain and simple.

Mrs. WATSON COLEMAN. Yes, they do.

Chief BEARY. I will answer the oversight—the comical, ironic part of this is in the State of Florida, as an individual I can buy a drone and I can fly it around and I can do what I want. As a law enforcement officer I can't operate one, because we have restricted them in Florida so anybody else can violate your privacy except the police. It is crazy, but that is what we have done because of the concern.

So right now there is no use of accountability that I am aware of.

Mrs. WATSON COLEMAN. Thank you.

Thank you, Mr. Chairman. I am really concerned about Orlando and Disney World.

Mr. PERRY. There are a lot of things to be concerned about. Thank you.

The Chairman now recognizes the Ranking Member of the full committee, Mr. Thompson.

Mr. THOMPSON. Thank you very much, Mr. Chairman.

Excellent witnesses. You raise a lot of, I think, interesting points.

For this committee, one of the real challenges is how do you insert the role of Government in this process? There are people who say, "Well, we have too much Government already."

But there are others who will say if something happens, "Why didn't the Government see this coming?"

So our question is—and I heard two things. Some say the role ought to be in DHS.

General, you kind of talked about a broader involvement, but with no head. You know, you said we ought to get everybody together.

So would your message to us be there is a role for Government, but somebody ought to have the primary responsibility for administering that role?

I will start with you, Dr. Humphreys.

Mr. HUMPHREYS. Yes, I do believe there is a proper role for Government here. This is a question of security and safety of the citizens, and it seems obvious to me that DHS should lead out on this.

There should be an interagency effort, but DHS should lead out on threats to our homeland, and especially so because the Secret Service, which has been highlighted in recent attacks at the—or intrusions at the White House, you know, is charged with protecting the White House and the President.

So having a head at DHS or standing up a committee, as Professor McNeal had recommended, I think is a good idea. They have got the expertise—or should have the expertise to lead this off.

Mr. THOMPSON. General.

General ROGERRO. Thank you very much, sir.

I would probably split it up a little bit and say, ''Department of Defense, you are responsible for those drones, if you will, or those remote-piloted aircraft that are state-sponsored.'' So those are the larger ones. Those are going to be more your Predators and Reapers.

As we talk drones, you know, it is very easy to slip into just thinking that they are just a quadcopter when they could be much more.

DHS certainly has a role in that and in the security piece, as well. So perhaps DHS is the right area.

Or do you pick an operational arm, such as in the Department of Energy, who has some very vital sites that they need to protect and could really identify the requirements and drive an effort and pull in all of those various bits on the defense as well as the mitigation technology and spread that throughout Government. So that is, perhaps, one solution as well, sir.

Mr. THOMPSON. Chief, you are on the ground. You talked about a lack of direction.

Chief BEARY. Right. A lack of authority. If we have one that we deem a threat, what authority do I have to take it down? It doesn't exist.

I think that Department of Homeland Security and DOD both share a role, and I think that in those areas of responsibility I think they could come back and make great recommendations for State and local law enforcement on how to deal with these threats.

Mr. THOMPSON. Doctor.

Mr. MCNEAL. So, as I mentioned in my written testimony, I think DHS should be the lead on this across all agencies. Of course, the threats exist in a lot of different places, but DHS has the experience to work with both the Federal Government and with local law enforcement.

I do have to dissent a little bit from Chief Beary's point on—well, not a dissent, but a nuanced point here, which is that if we think about the risks that law enforcement is worried about we must also recognize Congresswoman Watson Coleman's point, which is that drones can be a form of accountability.

What we saw in Ferguson was that local law enforcement—the AP got—FOIA'd these documents; local law enforcement asked for the grounding of drones so that the media couldn't cover what the police were doing. So it was used as—the security threat or the risk of safety to the officers was used as a tool to keep—to remove public accountability.

I think that type of thing is something that when we elevate the threat picture too high and we spread it too far across Government, we run the risk of allowing those types of things to happen. That is why I think a single point of responsibility and accountability is the best way we can ensure that we are not going off the rails with any particular policy preference from one agency or one law enforcement perspective.

Mr. THOMPSON. Thank you.

I yield back, Mr. Chairman.

Mr. PERRY. Thank you, Ranking Member.

Chairman now recognizes gentleman, Mr. Loudermilk.

Mr. LOUDERMILK. Thank you, Mr. Chairman.

Appreciate the testimony here, and I think, Dr. Humphreys and Dr. McNeal, you kind of hit on some significant areas with risk analysis as we go forward. Especially, I think the two categories that we can really look at this is the unintentional and the intentional.

Unintentional, we can mitigate some of the incidents with that via regulation, legislation, technology, et cetera. But the intentional—it is more difficult because the bad guys are going to be bad guys. They are going to work around that.

I put a lot of thought into this as an aviator, and working in search and rescue and different areas such as that. This is a question to anyone on the panel that has the information: Have there been any efforts or have we classified UAS platforms based on their technology, sophistication, payload capabilities complexity of operation?

Do we have a classification, like we do with civilian aircraft? You know, we have the different classifications—single engine, twin, land, sea-capable, et cetera.

Mr. MCNEAL. Congressman Loudermilk, we do not currently. However, I and a bunch of other experts in the field and manufacturers are working with NASA to develop a system, and testing is beginning in August. So from drone manufacturers to drone consulting companies, we are all working with NASA to create the system to certify and basically create those categories of capabilities for platforms.

The long-term vision is that once you have those categories—let's say class one through class five of small, unmanned aircraft—that will then ultimately feed into the unmanned traffic management system that we are hoping to have in place 10 years down the road. So it might be the case that——

Mr. LOUDERMILK. The next-gen?

Mr. MCNEAL [continuing]. That 10 years from now we will have something that is integrated with next-gen that will tell us the classification of aircraft. But that still won't do anything for home-builts that don't want to play ball with the traffic management system.

General ROGERRO. Congressman, actually NATO is already—does have a classification and it is based on weight. That does go class one up to class four, and then it also is classed by capabilities, and then what their top vulnerabilities as well as their top capabilities are in there.

So that is, once again, it is a good idea to look towards international partners instead of reinventing the wheel every time.

Mr. LOUDERMILK. General, the classifications, are you going from, you know, what you can buy at the kiosk at the mall, which are the basic indoor—a nuisance more than a threat type system, all the way up to the—those that require a landing strip—you know, take-off and landing?

General ROGERRO. Correct. It would go by—it would take things into account such as size, engine capacity, fuel or battery requirements, and their ensuing capability to speeds, et cetera.

Mr. LOUDERMILK. Payload?

General ROGERRO. Absolutely, sir.

Mr. LOUDERMILK. Okay. It sounds like there has been a—we are kind of in the same direction.

Looking at the unintentional side, as a private pilot the concern is those that can go, you know, above 500 feet AGL, especially around an airport. We have got plenty of class G airspace in the Nation, which is unrestricted, but yet a lot of private pilots, sport pilots, ultralight pilots operate at low altitudes but still at the slow speeds that we are flying, as compared to our military friends.

Still you are not going to see one of these quads or certain UAVs until after you have impacted it. Looking at this classification—model rocketry ran into this back many years ago and the industry kind of self-regulated itself.

If you are familiar with model rocketry, you can go to a hobby store and buy the little SDs model rocket engines. They are capable of low-altitude flight, but there is a classification that if you get above I think 1,000 feet and then 10,000—they have level one, level two, level three—you actually have to be licensed to purchase the propeller.

Has anybody looked at any type of classification that if a UAV is capable of a certain altitude, or outside-of-line-of-sight operation, then you have to be licensed? I fully think that if you are going to do that you need to at least have a basic ground school. Maybe not a medical, but at least know the area you are operating in.

Is there any movement in that direction?

Mr. HUMPHREYS. I will say that the challenge here is that the same drone that can operate up to 400 feet can easily operate above that, and even if we put in these geo-fences that exclude them from sensitive areas or from above 400 feet, an operator who had some knowledge of the autopilot system could override that sort of a geo-fence.

So the classifications smear into one another, and it is not just a question of knowing how high they can fly because most of them can fly fairly high if their batteries will hold out.

Mr. LOUDERMILK. What about technologies such as those that are beyond just the small quads you get at a mall—a requirement of a transponder or a next-gen system to be on those?

Mr. MCNEAL. The FAA has not required this type of technology but the industry is evolving to create it. So I recently saw ADS–B small enough to fit on a small, unmanned aircraft and it would interface with the, obviously, with the air traffic system, and you would be able—presuming that you are in an aircraft where you are then able to know other aircraft around you, you would know that that aircraft was nearby.

Of course, that doesn't solve the small sport and ultralight category of pilots who simply are not going to see this type of aircraft in the National airspace.

Mr. LOUDERMILK. Chairman thanks the gentleman from Georgia.

The Chairman recognizes the gentleman, Mr. Richmond.

Mr. RICHMOND. Thank you, Mr. Chairman.

Thank you, to the Ranking Member of the full committee, and the Ranking Member of the subcommittee, and the witnesses.

Let me just start with some very basic stuff.

Major General Roggero, let me start with you.

I represent the district with probably the largest petrochemical footprint in the United States on the Mississippi River in New Orleans, around New Orleans. Is there any technology out there right now that would prevent these drones from being used to do reconnaissance missions just to look at the security on these chemical facilities or our port or any of those very sensitive properties?

General ROGERRO. From a technology aspect, depends on what equipment they are using. But for a good amount of it I would say yes, there is technology that could do things.

I am not looking at policy right now or questions on technology, but yes, technology could get into the signal—either the video or the command and control of the system—and affect the navigation of the system so it may not be looking exactly what they want it to look at. So that is there.

But there are complications with that in terms of policy, with FCC rules and other things that—another issue that is out there is that the FAA has declared that all of these are aircraft, and as such, their second and third order of effects—perhaps unintended effects—but that aircraft is given protections as if it were a manned aircraft, as well. So there are certain actions, according to policy, that you can't take against them.

Mr. RICHMOND. Very quickly, I mean, part of this, I think, will have to be some industry, some Government, and everybody uses some common sense. But I think back to the very simple analogy of, if you go to the fancy golf courses and you are in the golf cart, there are some places the cart will not let you drive, like close to the green and other places they don't want you.

So at some point, you know, when we start talking about high school football games or, well, facilities—football stadiums, and baseball stadiums, and all of those things, do you see a day where those will, either GPS or otherwise, just be off-limits in terms of the capability of not being able to go in that space?

Dr. McNeal.

Mr. MCNEAL. Congressman Richmond, I don't necessarily see it as a technological solution. I think, as Dr. Humphreys pointed out, that is part of the equation.

In fact, the industry is already self-regulating for airports and other sensitive sites. There are start-up companies now that are allowing individuals to file the GPS location of their private property in the hopes that the manufacturers will then use those maps as no-fly zones.

I think what we will eventually find is that State and local government, through their zoning authority, will begin to say that certain areas are no-fly zones. We already see this in Los Angeles, for example. You are not allowed to fly a model aircraft on the beach or in parks. The National Park Service has said the same thing.

Then what happens is that local law enforcement can come in and say, ''Listen, this is a place where you are not allowed to fly,'' and they are able to intercept the individuals.

What that does for us from a security perspective is then it— when an aircraft is in that area, law enforcement doesn't have to make a judgment about whether it is nefarious or not; they can begin with the presumption that this person at best is someone who is unaware that they are violating the law in that particular no-fly zone, thus giving them reasonable suspicion or even probable cause to go talk to the operator. Then from there, that also puts— heightens the security picture for them.

Of course, there is a cost associated with that in that we lose some of the beneficial—the benefits of the technology. That is why I almost think that on designating no-fly zones that are non-Federal, we want to leave that up to State and local to figure out the right way to balance the costs and benefits.

Mr. RICHMOND. Chief, let me just ask you a question, because earlier you mentioned, you know, at some point you would have to make a decision whether to take a drone down or not. Let me just ask you the—for me, the practical part of it. How do you do that?

Let's assume it is over a high school football game and you can't determine whether it is a amateur hobbyist or whether it is something nefarious. If you decided you wanted to take it down, what do you do?

Chief BEARY. Well, therein lies the challenge. Most State and local law enforcement have no capability to do that.

No. 1, we don't have the technological capability. More importantly, we don't have the lawful authority.

As the general said, those are—they are aircraft. I don't have the lawful authority to take down an aircraft. There is not a State and local law enforcement agency in this country that does.

So right from the start we have no authority, so how am I going to respond?

These are the incidents, though, that the rank-and-file watch commanders in our agencies across this country are dealing with every single day now. When you have a hostage situation or you have any kind of major scene, you have got drones everywhere, and the helicopter is calling down saying, ''You have got to get these drones out of the airspace because I am trying to work a perimeter here.''

So our people have just—we don't have the resources and we don't have the backing of the law to help us deal with these situations. That is why I said in my testimony this is really a call for help.

Mr. RICHMOND. Mr. Chairman, thank you so much.

Thank you, to the witnesses.

Mr. PERRY. Chairman thanks the gentleman from Louisiana and recognizes the gentlelady from California, Mrs. Torres.

Mrs. TORRES. Thank you so much, and thank you for the opportunity to discuss this very important topic.

Just to follow up on your conversation, as a former 9–1–1 dispatcher I can tell you from personal experience that trying to get clearance to—as we are pursuing a vehicle, or our officers are pursuing a vehicle, trying to get clearance from an airport to follow a vehicle into that restricted zone, our helicopters are unable to continue that pursuit, but yet the media or, you know, folk from the ground can continue that pursuit through a drone.

That poses, you know—it is a very scary environment for those of us who live near an executive airport, for example, where our homes are very close by, and the—and these executive aircraft are landing—their landing route is right over our home. I thought, you know, birds were the scariest things that, you know, could face an aircraft as they are beginning to land, but now we have more and more of these drones that are getting in that way.

My question is really going to be to Professor Humphreys, and that is, in your prior testimony before the committee in 2012 you spoke of the use of civilian GPS and their ability to be spoofed or counterfeit. Can you tell me how technology has evolved? You know, what are the differences between then and now with older and newer models?

Mr. HUMPHREYS. Well, despite the passage of 3 years and despite the fast-moving technology in this area, you still cannot purchase over-the-shelf anything that can resist a spoofing attack like the ones we generate in my lab. I know the DHS has established some contracts to study the problem, and the FAA put together a tiger team to look at the problem, but still, only 3 years later, the problem exists.

In the current situation you can almost look at that weakness of GPS as a possible way to bring down these drones. But I would discourage that, because in transmitting false GPS signals, that will have unintended consequences for these executive airports, as you say. You don't want to endanger commercial airliners or even passersby who are trying to use their sat nav in their car to find their way to their office.

Mrs. TORRES. Thank you. I yield back my time.

Mr. PERRY. Okay. Chairman thanks the gentlelady.

We are going to go for a second round and we are going to go a little bit out of order. Mr. Loudermilk has to leave early.

So, as a matter of fact, I think I am just going to turn the floor over to him for questioning, and then we will move through the regular order at that point.

Mr. LOUDERMILK. Thank you, Mr. Chairman, for your indulgence. I do have a meeting to get to, but this is fascinating. It is of great interest to me and something that my office has been putting a lot of work and thought into.

What percentage of the platforms are manufactured domestically versus internationally? Do we know that?

Anyone?

Mr. HUMPHREYS. I know that the most popular quadcopter in the world is manufactured in China, and that is the most popular by far. But other U.S. domestic drone manufacturers—notably, the—robotics community, the do-it-yourself community are also large. As I said earlier, the knowledge is out there; the documentation is extensive.

Mr. LOUDERMILK. Okay. One of the reasons I was asking, you know, what level of regulatory constraint that we can put on the technology or, back to the police chief's ideas of how do we bring down these platforms when they are operating nefariously or unintentionally?

Is the technology there? Do we have the influence over the technology that we can—I imagine most of them use some type of R.F. signal to control them—to intercept the R.F. signal, to force a go-home activity, you know, fly back to the source? Is that even a conceivable idea that would be made available to law enforcement?

Mr. HUMPHREYS. It is conceivable. It does work. but it only really works against the unintentional, accidental, or unsophisticated attackers. If I am a sophisticated attacker I can adapt the autopilot to simply disregard any communication from the ground and work on an autonomous approach.

So it depends on what you want to protect. If it is just the accidental, incidental, yes, that can be effective.

But again, these technologies are operating in popular communication bands—wi-fi bands, and in the future they will be operating over LTE bands. You don't want to mess with those bands in a wide area. You will disrupt other people's activities, and maybe safety of life activities.

Mr. McNEAL. Congressman, the only thing I would add there is that while the interdiction problem seems—it seems problematic to us for the moment that it is there, and I can only imagine law enforcement having that feeling of helplessness, my response would be, you know, wait 25 minutes because the battery is likely to run out on that system, and there really are not very many systems in the quadcopter space that can fly for longer than 25 minutes. When you get into the fixed-wing model aircraft, basically, you get a bit more—a bit longer flight time.

The only other thing that I think I would raise there are the obvious civil liberties concerns and First Amendment concerns, because if you—instead of thinking of these as mere flying aircraft, if you think of them as flying cameras that might be operated by Fox News or NPR, you are immediately running into the question of the Government being able to turn off CNN's cameras, and that could be really problematic. So I am not certain that even if were able to implement this mitigation technology to take control of the aircraft, that it would be something that we would want to do.

Mr. LOUDERMILK. That is a good point. I agree with you there.

I also look at it from a personal privacy standpoint. What if it is hovering over my backyard, you know? What rights to do have to take it down? I have got a 12 gauge that could assist in that pretty readily.

But you can't engage that in a public area.

Chief, you brought up a challenge that you have. You have no right to take down any aircraft. No one in the Nation does, as far as local law enforcement.

But the operator is on the ground somewhere. You do have authority over the operator, correct?

Chief BEARY. The answer to that is "it depends." If they are lawfully in a place where they are allowed to do that—here is where we get into the question is, how do—who do I justify to what my actions were? Usually it ends up being in a civil court several years down the road.

That is why if we had some guidance on the front end it would help us write those policies for our personnel. Those are these situations we get into right now.

It is interesting you talked about your backyard, because what law enforcement is receiving now, we are getting those calls from the people that are on their back deck and then there is a camera in a drone looking at them. They call law enforcement, and what right do I have to deal with that?

As these systems get more sophisticated, as I talked about, with the flying by virtual reality, they are not—the people aren't as easy to find anymore, trying to find the operator.

Mr. LOUDERMILK. Right.

Chief BEARY. So it is problematic. We are seeing more and more of those privacy concerns coming it from residents that walk outside and there are three of them in their backyard.

Mr. LOUDERMILK. Thank you.

Thank you, Mr. Chairman.

Mr. PERRY. Chairman thanks the gentleman.

Chairman recognizes the Ranking Member, Mrs. Watson Coleman.

Mrs. WATSON COLEMAN. Thank you. Thank you, Chairman.

I want to thank each and every one of you for the information you shared today. You have given us a lot to consider, and hopefully we come up with recommendations and considerations that are cost—you know, that make sense in terms of cost, make sense in terms of application, make sense in terms of collaboration, and make sense in terms of the parameters that we—that get established in dealing with this sort of wide spectrum of issues.

My last question is to Mr. Roggero, because in your prepared testimony you recommended that on-going research and development program to devise counters to new drone technologies that should be established and funded.

So my two-part question is, regarding that funding, what type of investment in counter-drone technology should Congress expect to make to realize the intended results? Would you suggest partnershipping with colleges and universities to conduct research and development in the areas of drone insecurity?

General ROGERRO. Thank you very much for the question, ma'am.

I certainly do agree with investing because, as we have seen, this hearing is different from the one that was 2 years ago, and different technologies and things are out there now. The next hearing that we have in a couple years is also going to change and evolve.

So the R&D needs to be spent now. We have to focus on the capability that is out there now and available and install that, put that in place where it makes sense for the Government to protect those critical infrastructure points now. But going into R&D certainly makes sense, and going into universities is great for those scanning of the horizons in the 5-year-plus so that we don't find ourselves behind again.

I would even go one more step. This might be a great opportunity for a public-private partnership with those corporations that are heavily dependent in their new business plans on the use of drones, such as Amazon, Google, and Apple, who have all professed to be very interested in this technology, but certainly the security and safety issues can hurt their business plan, quite. So they may be a willing partner in this R&D as well.

Mrs. WATSON COLEMAN. Well I can certainly see that they are a natural partner here. Do you have any estimates of what you think the Government's cost associated with taking on such an endeavor would be? Just sort-of an estimate?

General ROGERRO. Well, I will turn to the university professor who is more engaged with grants than——

Mr. HUMPHREYS. Sure. So you can do a lot of good with very little funding in this area.

Mrs. WATSON COLEMAN. We are finding that out.

Mr. HUMPHREYS. I would say that you do need to recognize that even a risk assessment, however, is a—it can be something or it does require funding. I mean, we were talking earlier about doing a risk assessment before spending any funds, but a risk assessment itself requires some research.

I was involved with a DHS risk assessment in 2011 where a bunch of us subject-matter experts were brought into a room, asked questions we poorly understood, and asked to vote. It was just appalling, in my view, that this was the procedure for determining whether there were real risks, instead of handing us some marching orders and giving us some funding to go out and find out really what were the answers.

By the way, I have friends at Google today who may be watching this proceeding who are interested in knowing how they could help, because they do have a business interest in securing drones from malfeasance and making sure that the drones themselves aren't the bad actors.

Mrs. WATSON COLEMAN. Thank you.

Thank you very much, Mr. Chairman. I am through.

Mr. PERRY. Chairman thanks the gentlelady.

I have got some questions continuing. I will start with the general.

Given the wide range of threats the UAS can pose, the creation of a DHS strategy on domestic UAS will be a crucial aspect in mitigating the threat. Or maybe it is not DHS; you postulated maybe it would be DOD.

I just wrote down FAA, DOD, DOE, Justice. There is no limit, probably, to the number of agencies that might or should be involved in a comprehensive strategy.

But let's just say you were going to write a strategy. You know, I have got 5 minutes, right, and you have got some of that, so give me the high points, maybe, if you could, General, about what you think is important regarding such a strategy.

General ROGERRO. Certainly, sir.

I would first of all, as we discussed earlier, identify the threats, identify what needs to be protected, and in all cases that may not be a thing—it may be a reputation, it may be a brand. The White House is a great example. The drone was no threat kinetically, but to the reputation of the United States Government to protect a key spot, it very much is very important.

So I would identify those priorities and then get the resources down right and figure out where you need to apply those resources today while you are doing that research and development tomorrow to get those capabilities moving. So it is a multi-prong.

In the mean time, you also have to look at all of those authorities that law enforcement needs, make sure the rules are clear, and have a whole roll-out campaign, a strategic communications campaign, if you will, to get to the public, to let them know where you can fly, where you can't fly, what the penalties are, and if you see something you need to say something.

Mr. PERRY. Thank you. Continuing, just if you can, General—and anybody else, I will start with the general—some examples, maybe, of some larger UAS above 55 pounds. The availability, the payload—I am trying to determine—and—for myself and maybe anybody watching or listening what really the potential worst-case scenario could or would be.

Then, you know, if you maybe classify that in terms—I guess we had a potential cyanide issue at the White House. It is in the news today. You put a container—a small container—of anthrax or ricin or something like that on even one of these small, less than 55 pounds—I think it certainly has the ability to carry that payload.

Can you paint a picture for us—maybe not necessarily a worst-case scenario, but an actual probable scenario or a possible scenario with somebody with that kind of malicious intent, what the capabilities that exist?

General ROGERRO. Certainly. I am an R.C. hobbyist myself, and there are some local hobby stores not very far away from where we are sitting here today in the District of Columbia that if you go into you can have an F–16 jet that is about as long as this table that has a turbofan engine and has fuel which is in and of itself an explosive. This will do probably 200 to 300 miles an hour and you need a small runway to take it off from. It could fly from a location just outside of the District of Columbia into the center of the District of Columbia within minutes.

So that is here and that is current, so don't want to scare you any more than that, sir.

Mr. PERRY. I think I can understand the potential, the possibilities.

Dr. McNeal, you want to weigh in?

Mr. MCNEAL. Congressman Perry, the example that the general pointed out actually, in preparation for the testimony, I tried to find the earliest example of someone on the internet talking about this type of thing and there was actually a researcher out of—it was either New Zealand or Australia who basically said—who wanted to create remote control cruise missiles using a similar system to what the general is talking about.

I mean, this is DIY technology and there is very little we can do to mitigate against that, and you are looking at a high-speed missile at a low altitude.

With regard to the dispersal threat, we have—I think you have probably been in the threat briefings where people talk about the unmanned aircraft as a threat dispersal—as a dispersal method. It is almost too cute by half, though, because if you really wanted to have a high impact with a WMD, first we have the problem of getting the WMD. But if you have anthrax, that is not the best way to do it.

Go to every Starbucks on every corner in the District of Columbia, sprinkle it into the sugar. Or put it in a sugar shaker on the roof of your car and drive around and you will impact a lot more people through that dispersal method than you would through the aircraft, which—right?

Now, this, of course, assumes that the enemy is smart enough to think these things through, and some of the guys who have got caught haven't been the brightest, you know, bulbs on the Christmas tree. But——

Mr. PERRY. Even if they are not, I mean, let's say they are smart enough to go to a sporting event where—a large stadium and fly it low over the crowd, almost within arm's reach, I mean—and maybe it has an impact on you or not, but which one of us wants to be the person that said, "Well, look, I got checked out and I was fine," you know, over the course of thousands of people in that—and, you know, you already talked—the chief has talked about panic setting in, people running across each other and down the steps and falling, and little children and older folks, and so on. I mean, you can picture the scene, right?

Mr. MCNEAL. Yes. Mr. Chairman, you have also highlighted the other challenge in our planning process, which is that the threat of anthrax being spread at Starbucks in the sugar is something that is not as tangible as the cameras picking up the drone as it flies in over the football stadium, and that psychological impact is also something that the terrorists would go for, but also that unfortunately drives policy in a way that is not probabilistic but is possibilistic.

Mr. PERRY. Would any of you folks here, depending on size, classification, are any of you advocating or recommending registration of some type towards ownership so that the, you know, as the chief said, you know, the aircraft that is flying—and, you know, his officers are all standing there looking at it, they can't do anything about it. Maybe they can't at that moment, but once maybe rules are set into place where it is illegal to do what has just been done, they can actually track down the perpetrator and link those two up so that we know what he is doing at X house and there is justification.

Is anybody advocating or has anybody thought about that, or what are the considerations——

General ROGERRO. The only way right now is through support groups such as the AMA, which pulls in modelists and has a set of rules and regulations that people voluntarily roll into.

44

I would not be opposed to registration for somebody that either buys or builds a certain size UAS with a certain capability. I don't see where anybody would have a problem with that, and putting that accountability into this system where these capabilities are going so high so fast I think is probably a good thing and well-deserved.

Mr. PERRY. To the chief, you know, we talked a little bit about law enforcement's role or the role of UAS with law enforcement in the context of civil liberties, but also in the context of using the asset to law enforcement's advantage for search and rescue, or maybe surveillance in a hostile situation, et cetera, and then juxtaposed that to State laws and the 10th Amendment.

Can you describe, generally speaking, what do you think the—at this point—the role of UAS is, the legitimate role of UAS in law enforcement would be? Just so we have a clear understanding of where—you know, how we can help you and how we can assist in—but at the same time make sure that everybody's privacies and civil liberties are maintained?

Chief BEARY. Yes, sir. We certainly are always concerned about the civil liberty aspect, and I echo that concern.

Where they would be very beneficial for law enforcement are those quick tactical situations where I have got—the example I could give you is a railroad car. We have got a derailment and I have got a situation. Well, it might be 20 minutes or 15 minutes before I can get a helicopter, but I can put up an unmanned aerial system in 3 minutes with a video camera with a live feed back and I can see where I need to immediately create my evacuation zone, I can—I am getting real-time data instead of waiting for the State police helicopter or somebody else to get there.

So those kind of very fast incidents would be a huge help to us. Again, we talked—in my testimony I talked about high-risk warrant service. The same thing—instead of a loud helicopter being up drawing attention, I could deploy a couple of small drones with video feeds so that we could know that the area is secure and our—and the evacuation is going as planned.

So those are just a couple of quick examples of how we could deploy this and keep the public safe and the officers safe. Reduce costs, by the way. Helicopter time is very expensive.

Mr. PERRY. Well, it is unless you are the Department of Homeland Security, and I think at our last hearing they paid about $22,000 or $23,000 an hour for their Predator time. As a helicopter pilot myself, you know, there are a lot of helicopter pilots that would love to charge that amount of money to do surveillance and they would make a pretty good buck at it.

Finally, let me conclude with this: Based on what you have heard today—you folks are, I think, recognized as having some expertise in—the field, and we are trying to craft a policy, a strategy, et cetera—do you have a recommendation, each one of you, regarding which agency—I know, you know, I have something in my mind, but which agency should take the lead on maybe policy formulation or execution, should the legislative bodies do that, and work out the strategy, you know, proposed strategy?

We will start with Dr. Humphreys.

Mr. HUMPHREYS. Sure. As I said earlier, Chairman Perry, I believe the DHS has the obvious role to play here.

But I would also say that if DHS proves to be an unwilling leader or an incapable leader then others could step in. Someone else mentioned the Department of Energy. I also think the FAA has shown itself to be quite competent in this area. They are mostly looking at threats to aviation, but the threats by aviation against our homeland could also be within their expertise, I suppose.

But most importantly, I would like to reiterate that simply saying we are going to throw together a risk assessment isn't free. So we end up needing to have a deliberate risk assessment.

I believe DHS should lead that off, but it might need to—I would say it would need to involve deliberate research, perhaps funded research, whether by universities, Federally-funded research and development centers, or private groups, where they can do a deep dive into the problem and not just be asked questions off the cuff that they might be poorly prepared to answer.

Mr. PERRY. Okay.

General.

General ROGERRO. Yes, sir. I would say in the policy realm that DHS probably has the correct knowledge and background to take the lead on the security piece. However, it would have to be very closely aligned, I think, with the FAA, which, as you know, is a safety of flight piece.

But by designing policy and security you could take that airborne asset, as we have been talking about this morning, and push that into an aviation safety incident. So I think that the FAA has to be there with their expertise of aviation on this process, as well.

Mr. PERRY. Chief.

Chief BEARY. Because we deal with DHS on a regular basis, most State and local law enforcement agencies, to me it is a natural, where we have those relationships built. The number of agencies that report to them I think make it conducive.

I do absolutely agree with the general that the FAA needs to be a part of it, because it is a huge part of it. But integrating with State and local law enforcement, I think DHS would be the right vehicle to do that.

Mr. PERRY. Dr. McNeal.

Mr. MCNEAL. Congressman Perry, here is a four-part plan for how I would put it together. I would direct that the under secretary for National Protection and Programs Directorate be the lead individual responsible for this across the Federal Government.

Second, I would allocate to that office funding for a program office that would have temporary personnel—probably contractors that report to NPPD. You would probably need $5 million to $10 million to stand up the office with personnel and be able to do testing.

Third, I would require that all other Government agencies have to play if they want to get paid. So if DOE wants to implement security measures at their facilities they better participate in the threat assessment process, otherwise the funding won't be allocated through the under secretary down to those pieces of critical infrastructure.

Then fourth, as a check against sort of empire and bureaucracy-building—not that that happens in the District of Columbia—I would allocate some funding to the homeland security centers of excellence, which are your research institutions, that could do similar threat assessments to check the work of the Government. I will tell you, if you put Dr. Humphreys and I together with, you know, a half-million dollar grant, we would do a lot with that money—probably more than many of the people in Government would do because we are cheaper.

So I think that four-part plan of outside independent look, you have to play if you want to get paid, and then a program office supervised by the under secretary, is the most effective way to move this forward. It is relatively small cost. I recognize funds are limited.

Mr. PERRY. All right.

Thank you very much, gentlemen. I thank you for your valuable testimony and the Members for their questions.

Of course, the Members of the subcommittee may have some additional questions for the witnesses and we will ask that the witnesses respond to those in writing. Pursuant to committee rule 7(e), the hearing record will be open for 10 days.

Without objection, the subcommittee stands adjourned. Thank you.

[Whereupon, at 11:33 a.m., the subcommittee was adjourned.]

www.ingramcontent.com/pod-product-compliance
Lightning Source LLC
Chambersburg PA
CBHW081123280526
45787CB00007B/2951